D1431236

SEQUOYAH

Leader of the Cherokees

SEQUOYAH:
LEADER OF THE
CHEROKEES

───── ★ ─────

by ALICE MARRIOTT

Illustrated by BOB RIGER

Landmark
BOOKS

RANDOM HOUSE · NEW YORK

FOR

Bill and Dick

Acknowledgments

To Cherokee friends, living and dead

Mrs. Mary Hogue, Chelsea, Oklahoma

Lacy Starr, Euchatown, Oklahoma

Minnie Mouse, Euchatown, Oklahoma

Rachel Mouse, Euchatown, Oklahoma

Fannie Jumper, Jay, Oklahoma

Della and George Owl, Cherokee, North Carolina

Norah Roper, Tahlequah, Oklahoma.

To Ballantine Books, for permission to quote
from "Greensleeves" and "The Wee Cooper o' Fife,"
which are included in *The Burl Ives Song Book*,
Ballantine, New York, 1953,
pp. 34–35 and 178–179.

Contents

SEQUOYAH

Leader of the Cherokees

1
The Cherokees

The Smoky Mountains hid behind the clouds,
and mists smoked up from the valleys below
the peaks. The Indians, standing on the crested
ridges, looked out and down. Here was the end

of their road. They had found a country that was right for them. Here the Forerunners settled, and centuries later their descendants, still living in the green and silver land that lay at the end of the trail, called those Forerunners the Old, True Cherokees.

Before the people came into the Smoky Mountains, they had journeyed long and far. The Cherokee road had stretched for thousands of miles. It had crossed an ocean and a continent. Traveling the road had been a matter of thousands of years, for the Cherokees and for their ancestors.

The journey began somewhere in Central Asia, perhaps on the eastern border of Inner Mongolia. From there the Indians had traveled always and always slowly to the eastward. When the Forerunners stopped along their way, they rested and stayed, perhaps for a century at a time. Then one morning a young man would rise, restless, and lead his people to the east again.

Somewhere in the course of the journey, the People, as they called themselves, turned to the northward. After that their wanderings took them north by east. In time, traveling very slowly since they went on foot, they came to the

4

narrow strip of sea which we know now as the Bering Strait. The water then, for this was twenty thousand years ago, was crossed by a rocky, hilly bridge of land. All that is left of the land bridge now are the dots of the Diomede Islands, stretching from Siberia to Alaska.

The first Indians to emigrate from Asia crossed the land bridge and stood, without realizing it, on the earth of a new hemisphere. And then, as slowly as the Indians had traveled eastward, they turned and wandered south.

South from Alaska they journeyed, along the Pacific Coast or through the corridors of the Cascade and Sierra Mountains. And south again, bearing to the east once more, and so across a state line that would not exist for further thousands of years, and into New Mexico. Perhaps some of the newcomers settled near Folsom, on the plains, where there were dense herds of a kind of bison that is now extinct. Certainly men hunted those ancient animals, and left the stone points of their spears embedded in bones that have by now fossilized and become stone also. Perhaps some of the earliest, ancient wanderers spent the winters in the caves on the southeast slopes of the Sandia Mountains and wandered across the flat between that mountain and the Rio Grande, where the city of Albuquerque sprawls now. Certainly the oldest tools we know of in the Americas have come from the Sandia caves.

Then again someone grew restless, one day, and the journey to the south and east was continued; across the desert of Sonora and Chihuahua and over the mountains into the great valley that is the heart of Mexico, and on beyond. Some of the travelers, first the Toltecs and then the Maya, settled in the central valley and built great cities and temples there.

The later wanderers must have seen the Maya structures and admired them, for afterward buildings patterned after those of Mexico spread over much of the southeastern United States. Certainly the earliest Cherokees knew something of Mayan religion and science.

When and why some Indians turned north again we do not know, and we have not yet been able to discover the exact path by which they traveled. Perhaps the population in parts of Mexico had outgrown the available farming lands. Perhaps there was an epidemic among the people. Or perhaps, and probably the most likely explanation of all, the Indians believed they had lived through a religious cycle and must move on and start a new period of existence elsewhere. They may have come north across the Caribbean Sea to the mouth of the Mississippi by canoe or raft; they may have toiled up the map on foot, as their ancestors had gone southward.

However they came, they made the journey not very long ago, probably about our year 1300 or a little later. With them these Indians brought the knowledge of their generations. They were neither stupid nor ignorant people.

To calculate astronomical problems, for instance, takes a good deal of mathematical knowledge, which the Cherokees had. Other members of the tribe used their mathematics to plan buildings and to lay out towns around central temples. Still others were less concerned with scientific thinking. They were men who were interested in farming: in laying out fields and drainage ditches, and in planning, planting, rotating and harvesting crops.

Still other early Cherokees were doctors, who learned to use herbs, together with prayer and fasting and bathing in running water, to heal

7

the sick and unhappy. And other men were priests, who led the worship of the people around an eternal fire which burned on the town altar. Nearly always the priests were also musicians. They were historians and instructors, too, for they kept the legends of the people and taught the young folk of the towns.

Some of the Indian women made fine pottery. Some of them wove cloth of hemp or milkweed fiber and decorated their finest fabrics with brilliant feathers. Women whose husbands were good hunters, or who traded their own craftwork to other families for deerskins, made moccasins and winter blankets for their families to wear. Whatever the people did, they did to music, for, like all Indians, the Cherokees sang. There were farming songs and weaving songs, love songs and songs to put the children to sleep. There were even songs to sing while the soup was boiling. The people moved to music all their lives.

And, like all Indians, the Cherokees preserved their history and customs and beliefs in their songs. No one, in all of the Americas, could read or write at that time. No one yet had found a need for reading or writing. They knew nothing of the wheel and its uses, either. And to all the Indians gold and silver were useful only for making jewelry. Their tools were mostly of stone; although they knew enough about copper to make rivets and join pieces with them.

It was the white men who came across the Atlantic Ocean who brought these ideas to the Indians. The Spanish, French, and English introduced writing and reading to the new lands as they conquered them. The Europeans brought many other ideas that were strange to the Indians: They believed that gold had a value of and in itself. They thought that some men were better than others because of the ways their parents lived and the material things those parents owned. They were convinced that the good land men walked on could be owned by one man—not shared by all.

Yes, the white men in their coming brought the Indians many strange things. They brought mumps and measles and whooping cough and tuberculosis and many other diseases, including the common cold. They brought guns to replace bows and arrows, and they brought their own laws to replace those by which the Indians had formerly governed themselves.

9

As the strangers spread over the country and met more Indians of more tribes, there was a great need for a way of speaking to one another. Each tribe spoke a separate language. Some of the languages were related to one another, about as closely as English and German and Danish are. Others were worlds apart and as foreign to each other as are English and Russian and Arabic. Finally a dialect of Choctaw, called Mobilian, came to be the trade language. Mobilian was so easy to speak that even the white men, let alone other Indians, could learn to string a few words together into elementary sentences. Trade Mobilian had practically no grammar; instead people used Mobilian words in whatever sentence order they were accustomed to.

And gradually, as time went on, the white men moved into the rich valleys of the Smoky Mountains, leaving behind them the great plantations of the coast and the Piedmont region. Here in the southern Alleghenies the limestone hills rose, almost bare of farming soil, rolling and abrupt against the sky. Hardly could a man find a level place on a hillside where he might build his house. With even greater difficulty could he find patches of upland soil large

10

enough to plant as corn fields, or the smaller fields where beans and squash would grow. Deer were being killed off or pushed back into the deep ravines between the mountains, so (although some Indians now raised the white men's sheep, cattle, and chickens) meat was scarce and hard for the hunters to find. No Cherokee was starving in the early 1700s; there was still food for all. But the Indians' food, and all the life it supported, had been greatly changed and shaped by the white men's ways.

Such great changes usually come gradually, and that was how they had come to the Cherokee Indians. Slowly, very slowly, all their ways of living had altered. They were reshaped in a pattern that was still in many ways their own and still was Indian, but that was not wholly or natively Indian either. One change had brought about another, and then another change had followed in its turn. The time was coming for the greatest change of all. The day was almost there when a Cherokee would teach his own people, and some members of other tribes as well, to write. And not only to write, but to write their own language, in their own way.

11

2
Sequoyah: The Lame One

The farm was on a hillside, above the river.
Lame Boy thought of the stream as a river, and
always called it that, but his grandfather said
it was only a creek. If Lame Boy wanted to see
a river, he would have to travel a day to the
west. Then he could see the broad Tennessee,
and see how much water it carried, compared
to the stream at home.

But Lame Boy hadn't seen the Tennessee to

the west or the Holston to the north, while he had seen the river that flowed by the farm. Therefore, until he was convinced by the sight of bigger waters, he continued to speak of the home stream as "the river."

It was all a piece of Lame Boy's personality, and Grandfather often reminded him of the fact. Lame Boy stuck to things. Usually he waited to be sure he was right about something, but right or wrong, once he made up his mind, he froze to his idea. "It's the Indian in him coming out," Grandmother once said. Lame Boy's father was white. Grandmother perhaps would have preferred an all-Indian grandson. At least she looked for any traits she could find in him to make the boy seem more Indian than he was.

Having a white father was in itself no disgrace among the Cherokees. Nathaniel Gist was a fine man, and everybody who knew him respected him. He had come into the Cherokee country from the north to trade. But Nathaniel was no pack peddler, to travel on foot with his small wares in a knapsack slung between his shoulders. Nathaniel Gist came from a leading Baltimore family, and his wealthy father had supplied him with fine merchandise and good ponies to carry the loads.

Nathaniel was in partnership with two other young men, both Virginians, named Richard Pearis and Thomas Price. Their trading post was set up on the Long Island of the Holston River. Everybody who could get there, white or Indian, came to the post to trade with the young men. Richard and Thomas were satisfied with themselves and their business, and were perfectly happy to stay at the post and take care of it. Not so Nathaniel. He wanted to see new country; to watch the rivers run between the mountains, and the mountains rise

Nathaniel Gist loaded his ponies with goods

and clutch at the sky. So he loaded his ponies with goods, mounted his blue mare, and set out along the winding trails that Indian feet had beaten out during the centuries the Cherokees had lived in the Overhill country of eastern Tennessee.

We do not know exactly what Nathaniel Gist took in his packs when he first went out to trade with the Indians. His own lists have been lost or destroyed long ago. But the lists and bills of lading of other traders have been saved and have come down to us, and so we can make a pretty good guess at the supplies the young man carried.

and set out to trade with the Indians

Guns and ammunition had been part of the white men's stock in trade in the Indian country since about 1700. They were bulky and heavy to carry, as well as expensive, so Nathaniel probably did not carry many arms. Whiskey was a standard trade item, but it was more for dealing with whites than with the Indians. The Cherokees, particularly, disapproved of it, and there were tribal laws prohibiting the traders from bringing whiskey to the Indians.

But Nathaniel had cloth, of course. Printed cotton was in great demand among the Indians in the southern mountains in the last half of the eighteenth century. Many of the deer whose skins the Indians had once used for clothing had been killed. Cotton was cooler in the summer and softer in the winter and more comfortable to wear all year round than deerskin, even if deerskins had been easy to get. So there were certainly bolts of India cottons in Nathaniel Gist's pony packs.

Then, too, he probably had smaller bolts of the silky-fine, velvet-soft, red and blue woolen broadcloth called strouding. The English town of Stroud turned out this beautiful material and gave it its name. Strouding was very ex-

16

pensive. Probably Nathaniel did not carry much of it with him, but surely he had some.

And naturally he had cast-bronze hawk bells, in many sizes, made in France and Italy. The Indians did not hunt with hawks, but they loved to hear tinkling sounds when they moved, so they trimmed their dance costumes with the bells, or hung them around children's necks, or made bracelets of them for the young women to wear. Bronze hawk bells, polished with wood ashes and scraps of buckskin until they shone— no trader would go into the Indian country without plenty of them. And he would take along a few small hand mirrors, too, fragile as they were, for the young men loved to look at themselves and to preen before their reflections.

But the bulk of the load, and beyond question the most important part of it, was made up of needles and knives and scissors, packed into bronze kettles of all sizes. The Indians could never get enough metal knives and "double blades," both of which cut straighter and better, and held a sharper edge longer, than any stone tools. As for the brass kettles, the Indian women were so delighted to have containers that did not break, seldom wore out, and were easy to

17

clean, that they soon gave up making pottery for themselves unless pieces were needed for use in ceremonies.

And probably Nathaniel took along some imported Dutch tomahawks, too. The early traders in Manhattan had noticed that when the Indians made peace with their enemies they buried the blade of a hatchet and then smoked a pipe. When war was declared again, the pipe was put away and the hatchet blade dug up again. After the whites came, there was more fighting than there had been before, so both ceremonies were repeated often. This seemed a waste of effort to the thrifty Dutch. They invented a combination implement, which had a metal blade on one side of a hollow handle and a pipe bowl on the other. This they called a "tomahawk," which sounded enough like an Indian word to get by. Tomahawks caught on well and became fashionable among tribes who had never seen or heard of the Dutch. By Nathaniel Gist's day, they were standard trade items.

If he had room at the last minute, Nathaniel probably dropped some hanks of glass beads

into his load to fill up the cracks. Glass beads
were heavy, and they were comparatively expensive—they represented a pretty big invest-
ment for a trader at that time. The beads had
to be shipped from Italy to England, where a
high duty was leveled against them. Then they
were shipped on to the Colonies, where the
traders paid another duty before the beads could
be landed at Boston or New York harbors.
True, the red and blue and orange and white
and black and yellow were pretty colors, and
the Indians liked them. But the Indians already
had beads of their own, made of ground shells,
and fresh-water pearls, and semi-precious stones,
and seeds and nuts. If anything was to be left
out of a trader's pack, it could be a string of
beads.

In return for the goods he carried south,
Nathaniel hoped to get hides, especially beaver
and muskrat skins, to be shipped back to England. If he had poor luck among the eastern
Indians, he might go west for a little way, into
the land we know as Kentucky, and pick up
deerskins and even buffalo hides from the western tribes. Sometimes a little washed gold dust

19

or a few small nuggets of the metal found their way into a trader's pack, but that happened seldom in the Cherokee country.

So, one day along in the spring, Nathaniel Gist left the Long Island of the Holston River and started south into the Overhill Cherokee country. He rode the blue mare and he led the two spotted, Choctaw-bred ponies. The ponies were tough, cobby, compact little creatures, willing to be led or ridden, and capable of carrying considerable loads. But the mare was a quarter English thoroughbred—Nathaniel rode her as a hunter back in Maryland Colony —and she was a saddle horse who would never carry a pack load. Later, probably, Nathaniel traded her off and rode another Indian-bred pony. But not when he started out, singing off key and at the top of his lungs about the Lady Greensleeves:

> Alas, my love, you do me wrong,
> To cast me off discourteously,
> And I have lovéd you so long,
> Delighting in your company.
>
> I bought thee kerchers to thy head,
> That were wrought fine and gallantly,

I kept thee both at board and bed,
Which cost my purse well favour'dly.

I bought thee petticoats of the best,
The cloth so fine as it might be;
I gave thee jewels for thy chest,
And all this cost I spent on thee.

Thy smock of silk, both fair and white,
With gold embroidered gorgeously;
Thy petticoat of sendal right,
And these I bought thee gladly.

Greensleeves, now farewell! adieu!
God I pray to prosper thee!
For I am still thy lover true,
Come once again and love me.

And after each verse he sang the chorus:

Greensleeves was all my joy,
Greensleeves was my delight.
Greensleeves was my heart of gold,
And who but Lady Greensleeves.

Nathaniel met his own Lady Greensleeves
on a later trip out from the trading post. She
was the daughter of a very important Cherokee
chief, and her Indian name was Wut-teh. She

belonged to the Paint Clan, which was a leading group in the Overhill country. Like all Cherokee girls of good family, she had been carefully brought up. Wut-teh had been taught to cook and sew, weave and spin, keep house and direct the work of the Negro slaves her father had bought from white traders. She had also been taught to pound corn for meal and hominy and to do her share of the work in the family garden. Besides learning to be a good housewife, Wut-teh had learned to sing and dance, and to take part in the tribal ceremonies that were given for and by the young women.

So she was a good match for the prosperous young white trader. And happily, Nathaniel was the friend of Colonel George Washington who, with the Cherokees, had helped the British defeat the French and their Creek and Choctaw Indian allies. Wut-teh could probably have fitted comfortably into her husband's family home back in Maryland. But Wut-teh was a Cherokee before she was anything else. The white traders had brought many changes into Indian life. But one change they could not bring. No white man could ever make any Cherokee willingly leave home.

Like most young people in love, Nathaniel and Wut-teh finally worked out a compromise. Wut-teh stayed on the farm in the Overhill country with her parents and brothers. Nathaniel traveled back and forth between his father's home in Maryland and his wife's in Tennessee, with stops each way at the trading post on the Long Island. It probably was about as unsatisfactory as the life of a traveling salesman and his family is today. But still, it was better than nothing.

In those days, what was called "marriage by tribal law," like the marriage of Wut-teh and Nathaniel, was an established practice on the frontiers. Usually such marriages were happy ones, and many of them lasted as long as the couples concerned lived. In any case, Cherokee children belonged to their mothers' clans and families, and whether their fathers were Indian or white the children had a real, recognized place in the tribe and in the world. We know from the records of the Gist family that Nathaniel later settled in Kentucky, and that at the time he moved his business there he had a white wife and children. We do not know if Wut-teh was alive then or not. Perhaps she was dead, for her son, the Lame Boy, is said to have visited his father's white family and to have been on good terms with his stepmother and half-brothers. But all that happened many years later, if, indeed, the visit took place at all.

And yet, it is barely 175 years ago since this story began. It is too bad we do not know more than we do about Wut-teh and Nathaniel. At the same time, it is surprising that we know as much as we do. In those days very few people could read and write. Most traders kept their accounts by drawing pictures. A man named Black Beaver was represented in the trader's books by a scratchy drawing of a beaver, with lamp black or soot rubbed into the outlines to make sure he was black. Underneath the beaver would be a drawing of a piece of cloth, with straight vertical lines to show how many yards Black Beaver had bought. Or there would be a drawing of a knife, with more straight lines to show how many knives had been purchased. Then, opposite the pictures of white man's goods, there would be drawings of tobacco leaves or deerskins or pearls. Lines would be drawn across the page from side to side to show when the goods had balanced out against each other.

If the bookkeeping of the time was as simple as this, we needn't be surprised that other records were not kept at all. There was no system for registering births and marriages and deaths, for instance, except in those cases when the ministers or vestries of churches made records for their own information. Cities and counties did not keep population records; there were very few newspapers anywhere, and since this story begins before the American Revolution broke out, there were naturally no state records because there were no states.

Because there were so few records, we do not know when the son of Wut-teh and Nathaniel was born. In fact, we aren't even sure if he was their only child or whether he had brothers and sisters. And we know little or nothing about the boy in the years when he was growing up— only the few things he told about himself, casually, talking with friends in his last years.

Long afterward, when he was a grown man, Sequoyah, The Lame One, reckoned that he had been born in the same year as the United States—1775. It might have been a year off, one way or another, but 1775 was close enough to the date, he thought. And since it is a convenient date for any American to remember, we may as well say that Sequoyah was born in the year when his father left the Cherokee country and returned to the northeast to help his friend General Washington fight against the British. It must have been a hard parting for Nathaniel and his Indian family. The Cherokee Nation had resolved to side with King George's men against the Colonists.

We do not know what The Lame One was called when he was very young, or whether he ever had another name as many Cherokee children did. From the time we first hear of him, he was called Sequoyah—which means The Lame One. Some people who knew him said he was given the name when he was about half grown. One of his Indian friends told that Sequoyah became lame because of an injury he received in a hunting accident. Another friend said the crippling came from "a white swelling sickness" of his knee joint. That sounds a little as if he might have had tuberculosis of the bone. Sequoyah himself never talked about his lameness or when it came to him. He seemed to think that other things were more important and more worth talking about.

26

In spite of the fact that he was half white, Lame Boy grew up just like any other Cherokee. At first his world was bounded by the big old log house on the hillside, and by what he could see down the slope and across the stream when he sat on his grandfather's lap, watching the world from the doorsill.

From that doorstep Sequoyah could see the

Lame Boy learned much from his craftsman grandfather

spring mists smoking up off the water and the flames of autumn-colored trees hurling themselves downhill to quench their brightness. He could see pieces of sky and moving white clouds, and he could see the clouds become gray and darken and turn purple-black when mountain storms came up. He could see the greeny-yellow blossoms of the sourwood trees, and the greeny-white blossoms of the dogwood, and the pinky-gray-violet of the redbuds, when their blooming seasons came. The air was perfumed with one scent after another, from the earliest honeysuckle and sourwood to the muscadine grapes ripening in late fall. For a little boy and his grandfather, the hillside was a rich place for just sitting and looking and breathing!

Sitting and looking was a very important part of Cherokee life, but it was only a part. There were times when grandfathers and little boys were very busy doing other things. Grandfather had plenty of work. He was a skilled and honored craftsman and worker, who made carved masks for the ceremonial dances, bows and arrows for the hunting men, bowls and spoons of wood for the women who stayed at home

28

and kept house, and toys for little boys when he had time to spare from other jobs.

Behind the log house there were two wood-piles. One was of ordinary oak and ash and hickory and pine; fresh-felled, split, and chopped in lengths that could be burned in the fire-place of the big room to cook the food and heat the house. The other woodpile was smaller, but it was made of wood that Grandfather had been collecting all his life. Whenever a load of firewood was gathered and dumped in the yard, Grandfather stacked it so that he would have a chance to handle every stick of wood separately himself. He examined each piece for straight-ness of grain or the roundness that showed the wood had been a burl, growing like a wart on the trunk of a tree. He stroked the wood to feel whether it "warmed" to his hand, which was his test of a piece that could be carved. A piece of wood that "stayed cold" Grandfather stacked in the fuel pile. It was good only for heating the house; it had no warmth for the heart unless it was burned.

The wood for carving was never allowed to touch the ground. Grandfather had made a sort of framework of sticks on which the woodpile rested, so that the air could circulate around every piece of wood. The pile was in the shade, for hot direct sunlight might warp the fine grain and make the wood worthless for carving. And every now and then the woodpile was shifted so that the wood which had been near the ground was raised to a higher level and that which had been most exposed to light was lower and shaded for a time.

Grandfather marked the end of each stick that went into the carving pile so he would know which pieces were the oldest and were ready to use. The picture of a beaver meant that the stick had been laid aside the year he and Grandmother were married, when they were especially busy building their house and furniture. The figure of a branch meant that the stick had been gathered a year later, when he and Grandmother planted their first garden. And so different objects marked the years right down to the one when Sequoyah was born. For that year there was a picture of a trader's pony on the end of each of four sticks to show that they were the same age as the trader's son.

Once Sequoyah asked his grandfather what

30

he meant to make of those four sticks. Grandfather put his head a little to one side in a way he had, and considered the matter.

"Well," he said, slowly, as he always spoke, "let's see. Here's a fine straight piece of hickory, with a good, even grain going along it clean from end to end. That will make you a hunting bow, when it is ready to work with and you are strong enough to pull it. And here is a round of white oak log that we can split into splints someday, to make housekeeping baskets for your wife when you marry. It's just about big enough to make her a full set. And here's a double ash burl—that will make you a bowl and spoon, and I can start working on them pretty soon now. And this is a single walnut burl—but a good big one—and that will make a bowl for your wife, big enough to serve hominy to the whole family. There! You see? I have a use planned for every one of your sticks, already!"

"No mask, Grandfather?" Sequoyah thought that the ceremonial masks were the most beautiful things his grandfather made. He wanted a mask; he very much wanted a mask. But where was the wood to make it?

"No mask," said Grandfather, more slowly

31

than he had ever spoken before. "No mask, Sequoyah. The son of a white man is not allowed to wear a Cherokee ceremonial mask. He is not all Indian."

"I am Indian! I am! I am!"

"Not all Indian," Grandfather repeated. "If you were all Indian, you would not get angry about it. You are part white man, and this anger proves it."

"I don't want to be a white man! I won't be a white man!"

"Sequoyah," Grandfather said, and now he spoke as sternly as a chief, "you are acting like a white man. How can you make people believe you are even part Indian, if you act this way?"

Sequoyah did not cry. White or Indian, boys do not cry. He stood with his hands doubled up until the muscles made knotted cords along the insides of his wrists, and his arms ached from holding them that way as his throat ached from swallowing the muscle-knot that choked him. But at last he got down the lump in his throat and a good big piece of pride with it, so he was able to speak.

"Maybe I'm not all Indian," he said, looking his grandfather in the eye—straight and rude as any white man. "Maybe I'm not all Indian." His eyes focused on the ground then, as a polite Cherokee boy's should. "But I can talk like an Indian and live like an Indian. I will—all my life. Hear me, Grandfather. Hear me, you trees in the woodpile. Hear me, my river. I—am—going—to—talk—and—live—like—a—Cherokee—all—my—days."

Growing up at Taskigi Town in the Overhill Cherokee country, it was easy to forget that white men existed, let alone that you were part white yourself. Sequoyah had a small bow and blunt-ended bird arrows that Grandfather had made for him, and he hunted through the woods and ranged across the hills. Usually he went out with the Raincrow boys, whose father's land adjoined Grandfather's. They were cousins of his on his mother's side, and he had the right to tease them, as they had the right to tease him. If any of the boys admitted that one of the others could hurt his feelings, he had betrayed their relationship.

It was his oldest Raincrow cousin who taught Sequoyah to use a blowgun, and to bring down the smallest birds with darts that were made of honey-locust thorns tipped with thistle down, with the points smeared with snake poison.

33

At first Sequoyah had trouble holding the ten-foot length of wild cane to his mouth. After he had learned to hold and balance the blowgun, he still had trouble. Uncle Raincrow had dropped live coals through the cane again and again, and shaken them around and around in the barrel to burn out the joints that separated the stem into sections. But no matter how carefully he worked, he left a little rim of pithy inside wood around each joint, and so the inside of the blowgun was slightly bumpy. If you did not know how to use it, you would find that your dart had caught on one of those rims and hung there.

The secret of shooting a blowgun was to hold it level, shoulder high, while you put the dart into the near end of the barrel. Then, with one quick, sure movement, you raised the tube to your lips and puffed strongly into the mouthpiece. The dart shot out of the other end of the cane, and if you were a good shot you hit the bird or rabbit you were aiming at. The great advantage of using a blowgun was that it made much less noise than a twanging bow string, and you could bring down game that was too small or shy to be taken in any other way.

34

Even though the Cherokees were wearing clothes made of cotton fabrics that had been imported from India by way of England, they still used feathers in making their ceremonial costumes and headdresses. Sequoyah slipped through the vine-tangled woods with his cousins, and they brought back woodpecker topknots and wild-turkey wing feathers and hummingbird breasts for Grandfather and Uncle Raincrow.

Sequoyah learned that he could stand still in one place—easing his lame leg by raising his foot on a log or a loop of vine—and wait for the birds to come within reach, instead of struggling through the woods to search for them. Once, when he brought back four ivory-billed woodpecker crests to Uncle Raincrow, Uncle offered to trade him something for them. Sequoyah was angry, as he had been angry the day Grandfather told him he could never have a mask.

"My father is a trader," he said furiously to his uncle. "I am a Cherokee." He left the feathers at his uncle's feet and limped back through the woods toward home. It was a long time before he could make himself walk out of the house and turn in the direction of his uncle's place again.

35

For days and weeks Sequoyah went around telling himself that he could never forgive Uncle Raincrow. This was the way, he thought, that tribal feuds started. Someday, perhaps, all the Cherokee tribe would be divided into two factions—the Sequoyah faction and the Raincrow faction. When strangers came to the tribe and asked, "What happened to divide this great nation in this way?" the answer would be, "Sequoyah was insulted by his Uncle Raincrow. Men of honor must follow Sequoyah."

Then he caught a cold.

Theoretically, Sequoyah should have had less trouble with a cold than the other Cherokees, for he was part white and the cold was a white man's disease. But the part of him that was Indian was the part that got sick, apparently. His nose and eyes swelled, he sneezed and blew and coughed, he was alternately hot and cold, he was restless and generally miserable and cross.

Wut-teh dosed him with sour wood-bark tea and bloodroot tea and sassafras tea. She put him to bed with a hot stone at his feet and a cold cloth on his head. She rubbed his chest and nose with bear fat, and she tried very hard indeed not to let anyone know that she was terrified to have her twelve-year-old son so ill. Grandfather knew, of course. Wut-teh was his daughter, and he could tell when she was disturbed. He took a rattle made of a gourd so old it looked as if it were coated with black wax instead of with time, and he sat down beside Sequoyah's bed to sing him well.

Usually Grandfather's singing was so beautiful that it would cure you to hear it. That particular day, though, Sequoyah was so wretched he didn't want to listen. When Grandfather sang the Hummingbird Song for the fourth time, Sequoyah turned over on his plank bed and pulled the homespun blanket up over his ears to shut out the sound. Grandfather finished the song as if he hadn't noticed anything—after all, his singing would all be wasted if he didn't sing each song four times. Then he got up, put his rattle on the mantel shelf, and walked out of the house. Without wasting time in talking to anybody, he went over to Uncle Raincrow's house, and when he came back Uncle Raincrow was with him.

Uncle Raincrow, naturally enough, did not know that he and Sequoyah had divided the Cherokee tribe between them in a great feud. All he knew was that one of his nephews was sick.

So he walked into the house and over to the bed, and stood looking down at Sequoyah, who by that time had thrown the blanket off.

"Feverish," said Uncle Raincrow, holding his hand out above the boy's head but not touching him.

Sequoyah twisted away from the hand and shivered as he stared at the log wall behind his bed.

"Chillish, too," Uncle Raincrow announced.

"Yes," said Wut-teh, "and sick at his stomach, and not hungry. All last night he had dreadful dreams, too—dreams about something eating him, I think, from the way he groaned."

Sequoyah jumped in his bed. He could not remember his dreams of the night before; sleeping and waking ran together in his mind, and he could not tell one state from the other. But dreams of being eaten were very important to the Cherokees. To dream of being eaten meant either that some supernatural enemy was attacking you or that some supernatural gift was coming to you. Without thinking about it, he spoke.

"I was being eaten up by a water monster," he announced. Being eaten by a water monster was something he had heard the older people talk

38

about in whispers. It might mean that the supernatural gift you were to receive was almost too
big to realize, and much too sacred and important
to talk about. Without turning around to look,
Sequoyah knew that Uncle Raincrow was impressed by the dream.

There was a long, hushed pause in the room.
Sequoyah could hear the hawk bells on Uncle
Raincrow's shirt tinkle as his uncle breathed. He
could hear the swish of his mother's skirt as she
moved to the fireplace, and he could hear Grandfather say a word under his breath. The word
was,

"Cherokee."

"He had better go down to the river," Uncle
Raincrow said finally.

Going down to the river was the Cherokee cure
for the ills of the body and the mind. It was also a
kind of initiation ceremony for young men, when
they outgrew their boyhood. And whenever a
person made a change in his way of living or
thinking or believing, he went down to the river
to wash away his former life and make himself
ceremonially clean for the new one. If Sequoyah
went down to the river now, it might cure his
cold, but it would also mark the beginning of his

39

grown-up life. It would make him worthy of the dream of being swallowed by the water monster if it were a good dream, and free him from it if the dream were dangerous.

Grandfather and Uncle helped him get out of bed, while Grandmother and Wut-teh built up a roaring fire in the fireplace. They made him strip in front of the blaze, and Grandmother handed him a new breechclout, made of fine, dark blue strouding. Then Grandfather and Uncle Raincrow, standing one on each side of him, sang four songs, each four times. The songs were prayers that he would get well, and they were also prayers that he might become a fine man, worthy in every way to be a Cherokee and a leader.

After the songs were finished, Uncle took his medicine pouch from the knot where it hung at his belt. Sequoyah had never seen Uncle Raincrow without the medicine pouch, although he had never before seen the pouch opened. Now he watched while Uncle Raincrow unfastened the knot that held it to his belt and loosened the string that closed the little, worn, old yellow buckskin bag.

Grandfather brought a gourd dipper of fresh

water from the spring above the house, and Grandmother brought a stone knife from its place on the mantel shelf beside the clock. Uncle Raincrow measured just enough dark brown powder from the sack to cover the point of the knife, and stirred it into the fresh water with the knife blade. Mother untied the knot of her bead necklace and dropped a blue, a white, a red, and a black bead into the mixture. Uncle handed the dipper to Sequoyah.

"Now," he directed, "drink it all down, and be sure you swallow the beads."

The beads had looked very small when they were part of a string—not nearly as big as the green peas that Sequoyah pulled from the vines and swallowed whole when he was weeding in the garden; nothing like as big as the wild grapes that he and the other boys swallowed by hand-fuls as they wandered through the woods. But knowing that the beads were there, and that they were hard, cold glass, and that they lay in the bottom of the dipper waiting to be swal-lowed, was frightening. Suppose the glass poi-soned him! That was silly. His own mother would certainly never give him anything to drink if it were poisonous.

41

He shut his eyes and tipped the dipper up until the rim rested against his forehead, opened his mouth and throat, and let the water pour down. He held onto the dipper for a full minute after he was sure everything it had held was inside him. Then he gulped and held out the gourd. Not until he felt Grandmother take hold of it did he open his eyes.

"Now!" said Uncle Raincrow again. "Now! Run for the river!"

With Uncle Raincrow loping on one side of him and Grandfather coming along, a little behind them, on the other, Sequoyah headed downhill. His lameness made him slightly uncertain on his feet, and weakness made him stumble once or twice, but he got to the bottom—to the river bank—without falling. His uncle and Grandfather took hold of him, each hanging onto an arm, and dipped him quickly under the water and up again, four times.

When he came out the final time they turned him around and headed him for the bank, where Mother and Grandmother were waiting with an outspread buffalo robe. They wrapped it around him, the fur tight against his body, before he had time to remember that the hide was one his

42

father had brought back from his last trip to the west. It had come from a prairie tribe, called the Kickapoo, far, far away.

Up the hill they all ran, to a small brush shelter on the south side of the house. The women had covered it tightly with robes and blankets, and built a fire outside its door. Grandfather went into the lodge and beckoned Sequoyah to follow him. Uncle Raincrow took a pair of forked sticks, and with them he rolled stones that had been heating in the fire through the door and into a hole in the middle of the lodge. The lodge roof was so low that even Sequoyah had to stoop. Grandfather was bent nearly double, but he took a bucket of water that Uncle Raincrow passed in to him and splashed it on the hot stones. Steam rose and filled the small space before Sequoyah could realize that his uncle had sealed the door from the outside.

"Stand over the stones and soak in the steam," Grandfather directed, and the boy obeyed.

Four times they renewed the stones and poured water on them, and four times the steam rose stifling. At last Sequoyah was too weak to stand, and he dropped down on a bed of willow branches that was laid against the wall of the

43

lodge. Then Grandfather struck the wall of the lodge with his fist, and Uncle Raincrow opened the door. Between them, the two men raised the boy by his arms and helped him back to the house.

Inside the house the fire was blazing brighter than ever, and there was a stack of homemade white cotton towels to be used by Sequoyah for rubbing himself down. Then, when he was clean and warm and dry, he fell into bed. Grandmother handed him a cup of hot squirrel broth, and he poured it down as he had the medicine. Before he knew whether he was hot or cold, Sequoyah was asleep. When he wakened at noon the next day, the cold was gone, all but a kind of weakness and limpness that lasted until he had eaten another meal.

After such an experience, which you would naturally think of as a turning point in his life, you would expect to be told that Sequoyah was a changed personality. He wasn't, since he was entirely a human being. He kept on hunting with his bow or his blowgun; he still didn't care a whole lot for corn-meal mush unless the corn had been parched brown before it was ground; he still wanted a mask as much as he ever had,

44

and he was as determined as ever to be all Cherokee all his life, in speech and deed.

The one big change that came along was that late in the summer, when the harvest was in, he was allowed to play in the ceremonial ball game with the grown men and the other older boys.

Once the Cherokees had thought of the ball game as a preparation for war. If a man could last a whole day through, running and jumping and striking others down with his club, he could last a whole day in battle, they said. Sometimes the men took their preparation for war so seriously that someone was badly hurt. Men had even been killed in the ball game. Every able-bodied Cherokee man was expected to participate.

For four days before the first game in which he played, Sequoyah stayed, with the other young men, in a special roofed open-sided shelter beside the great ceremonial grounds. At one end of the grounds was the pile of ashes where the town's eternal fire burned, guarded day and night by priests who kept it alive. Here the tribe held the all-night ceremonies that marked the planting, the harvest, and the nights of the full moon. The other end of the grounds was the ball field.

45

Every able-bodied Cherokee man was expected to participate in the ceremonial ball game

In the shelter, the young men talked and slept. The older ones smoked sometimes—long, cane-stemmed pipes with small, round stone bowls. The old men talked to them about Cherokee history and customs, and brought them bowls of unsalted mush.

Every morning and every evening two old men carried a steaming pottery jar into the shelter, each of them holding it by a stick passed through its loop handles. The jar held about five gallons of liquid made by boiling roots and herbs with the trailers of the wild smilax vine. Each young man went forward separately and emptied a dipper of the bitter black drink. Then he went aside, to a place where clean white sand had been spread out, and vomited. When he came back to his place, the old men scratched his arms and legs with a seven-toothed comb of thorns until the blood ran.

After the young man was cleaned out, and the bad blood had left his body, he went down to the river to swim. Then he came back to the shelter and lay down. Only when the young men were thoroughly, ceremonially clean, could they take part in the game.

On the morning of the game itself, the old

men brought the jar containing the black drink to the shelter before daylight. The sky of the east was turning white along the horizon, but the stars still showed whiter than the daylight against the black-blue of the upper sky. And every one of the young men was clean and empty when the sun rose, and they all stood in a long line, facing east, to sing it up to its place in the sky.

Then the old men opened the door of a little house beside the shelter where the younger ones had waited during the four days. The old men took out the ball clubs—long, slightly crooked sticks with sinew nets covering their looped upper ends—and handed two to each player. Then the young men trotted out onto the ball ground and gathered around a post that rose high above their heads in its center. A carved wooden fish swam against the blue of the sky on the top of the pole.

The men from the Red war clans gathered on the north and those from the White peace clans on the south. They were silent, waiting, for what seemed to Sequoyah like a whole day, before Uncle Raincrow threw a small buckskin ball into the air, turned, and ran back to the sidelines. Before he was well away from the pole, a young man on the Red side had caught the ball between his two netted sticks and was off down the field toward his goal. All the others pounded after him, the White players trying to get the ball away from the runner with their own sticks, and the Red ones trying to block them and stop them.

Sequoyah could not run as fast or as well as the others, but he ran. All day he ran, back and forth, up and down the field, trying to follow the ball and its movements, trying to block the Red players when his own side had the ball, trying to stop the opponents and give the faster White runners a chance when the other side took it. They could use their bodies and sticks to block other players and catch and carry the ball, but a man who used his hands was penalized.

Behind and beside Sequoyah, at the edge of the field, he knew the women and girls and the older men were cheering and shouting. Probably they were betting, too. The year before, it passed through his mind as he ran, he had bet his bow and arrows on the White side. He had won then. Let them win again! Powers Above, please let us win again!

49

Once he stumbled over a player who was lying knocked out, flat on the ground. The next time the play came back that way he thought he saw the boy sitting up on a blanket, off the field, with a white bandage wound around his head. Not until the game was over did he find out that it was his cousin The Tassel who had been hurt, or that Wut-teh was the one who had run onto the field and dragged the boy out of danger before the pack could trample him again.

It was sundown before Uncle Raincrow ran out onto the field and hit the pole four times with his war club to show that the game was over. He held up a white flag and waved it, to show that the peace side had won. All the young men gathered near him, singing, and Uncle led them back to their shelter. There the old men waited with their pot of the black drink, and there all the young ones drank it and vomited for the last time.

Sequoyah limped home. He was empty and hungry, and he ached in places he had not known were parts of his body. But he was relaxed, and even when he sat by the fire too tired to eat the bowl of stew Grandmother handed him, just holding the bowl in his hand until it began to slip away from his fingers and Wut-teh took it and pushed him into bed, he was happier and easier in his mind than he had ever been. He had played the Cherokee war game with the others, like a real Cherokee. He might never wear a mask in a ceremonial, but he had proved that he belonged to his Nation.

3

The Craftsman

Perhaps it was because Sequoyah was accustomed to seeing Grandfather work with wood, or perhaps it was because his own hands shaped themselves naturally around any tool he touched. Anyhow, he never thought of making his living in any way but as a craftsman. The Cherokees had always been fine technicians; they had worked in wood and clay, in shell, and in many semi-precious stones for centuries. Some of the

tribesmen had even traded with the Iroquois na-
tions, their kinsmen to the north, for raw copper
from the shores of the Great Lakes, and had
learned to hammer the metal into jewelry for
themselves and their wives.

It was part of resolving to be a Cherokee and
nothing but a Cherokee that the boy learned to
use tools; first the saw and hammer and adze
that Grandfather used in woodworking, later
other tools for other crafts. By the time he was
fifteen, he could split board from logs, driving
a series of wedges into the wood to section it, and
he could split "shakes" to shingle roofs. Shake-
splitting was highly skilled work, usually en-
trusted to grown men. One way of doing it was
to soak a white oak log in water until its bark
could be peeled off easily. Then the craftsman,
using small wedges, separated the growth rings
of the log and peeled off each year's growth in a
single sheet. Each sheet could then be split into
shingles of whatever size he needed, or could be
cut into the narrow strips, called "splints," that
many eastern tribes used to make their household baskets.

When Sequoyah was sixteen, he made a chair
and sewing table for his mother. The next year,

at seventeen, he built her a loom room, working single-handedly until the roof was on and the floor laid. Then he set about to build her a new loom, strong and fine enough to weave cotton cloth for shirts and aprons. Since the English had lost their war with the Colonies, imported fabrics were harder to come by, and more and more people wove the cloth for their clothing at home.

Now it was perfectly possible to put a loom together with wooden pegs, and to use no metal at all in building it. The walnut loom on which Grandmother wove rag carpets and heavy sacking was made that way. But when fine cloth is being woven for dresses and shirts, the threads that go into it must be beaten close together, and a loom that is set with metal can withstand the pounding of the batten better than one that is pegged with wood.

No one who lived near Taskigi Town could be called a skilled metalworker. One or two men had learned to do the heaviest, crudest kind of blacksmithing on their own places and for their neighbors, but none of them was able to make the bolts and parts to set a loom. Sequoyah watched for a while, as first one and then another of his neighbors showed him how to hammer out square nails or to shape horseshoes. Then he turned his back on his home town in the Overhill country, and, with a sack of ham and parched corn on his shoulder and his old liver-and-white spotted hound dog at his heels, he headed downhill for the Valley towns to learn blacksmithing.

Life in the Valley towns was much more exciting than life in the Overhill country. Here travel followed the streams; not only did boats go along the rivers, but trails that were almost roads wound beside them. Here were houses painted white—houses with floors entirely covered with rugs, and separate rooms for cooking and sitting and sleeping. People had horses and wagons down in the Valley towns, and some of them had closed-in wagons called carriages. The white Christian missionaries had built a church and school at Spring Place, Georgia, and were teaching the Indian and part-white children who were sent to them for schooling.

Now Sequoyah learned for certain that he was not the only part-white Cherokee in the world. Other people, boys and girls and men and women, had white fathers. Some, like young John Ross whose father kept the ferry and land-ing near Spring Place, had white grandfathers on both sides of their families. Yet John Ross had an Indian name—Cooweescoowee, The Great White Bird, he was called. Ross spoke Cherokee as easily as he did English. He hunted with a bow and arrow or a blowgun almost as well as Sequoyah did himself. Perhaps, Sequoyah thought, if your white father were rich, and if he stayed at home most of the time, you could make the most of both the worlds you had been born into.

Well, thinking about the Ross family and puzzling about his own would get him nowhere, he decided. He thought about these things only in the cracks of time he found between his jobs as a blacksmith.

Iron was good to work with. Iron gave a man something to drive at, and iron returned a blow for each blow he gave it. But iron was coarse, and in a sense it was crude. After Sequoyah had learned to make the parts for Wut-teh's loom, and had taken them home, built them into the loom, and bolted the loom to the floor so it would be steady in its place no matter how hard the batten drove home, he was ready to learn to do something else with his hands.

In the old days, as he well knew, the Cherokees had wrought with copper. He could not find raw copper to work with, but he did find first one woman and then another with a copper kettle that needed mending. Copper was a problem, all right. It would not fuse, as iron did, if he heated and hammered it. It got brittle; the edges he was trying to weld crumbled and broke, and the hole he had started to mend got larger instead of smaller. He solved his problem by soldering a patch over the hole, but then the kettle got hot when it was hung in the fireplace full of hominy to be cooked for dinner, and the heat melted the solder and the patch fell off. Sequoyah finally learned from a traveling English tinker how to patch a copper pot by riveting a piece over the hole. But copper was hard to work with, and copper was not for him.

It was that same Englishman who showed him the metal that felt right to his hands, and that he could use. They sat under a chestnut tree, beside a spring, smoking their pipes after lunch. The hound lay beside Sequoyah, with his nose pointed toward his master, and the Englishman was humming, half under his breath, "The Wee Cooper o' Fife":

There was a wee cooper wha lived i' Fife,
Nickety, nackety, noo, noo, noo,
And he had gotten a gentle wife,
Hey, Willie Wallacky, ho, John Dougal,
A lane quo rushity roo, ro, ro.

She wouldna card, she wouldna spin,
Nickety, nackety, noo, noo, noo,
For the shamin' o' her gentle kin,
Hey, Willie Wallacky, ho, John Dougal,
A lane quo rushity roo, ro, ro.

In his hand the tinker held the silver shilling Sequoyah had paid him to learn to rivet copper, and as the Englishman sang, he tossed the coin up and down, back and forth, from hand to hand. At last he held it out on his palm.

"You can work with this," he said, using the trade Choctaw called Mobilian that had spread over the face of the country wherever the white men went.

"How?" Sequoyah asked, looking at the shilling while he reached out with one hand to pull the hound dog's ears. He, too, spoke Choctaw. He was keeping his promise never to learn to speak English.

An English tinker showed him how to patch a copper pot

"Work it like iron. Heat it and pound it. Metal's metal, boy. If you can learn to work one, you can learn to work all or any of them."

"Except copper."

"Even copper. Finish your pipe, and I'll show you."

The pipe was new, and Sequoyah hadn't been smoking long. He knocked out the charred tobacco and the last sparks on the bare earth, and when he got to his feet he put his heel on the last of the fire, for fear of starting a bigger blaze and making trouble in the woods. The Englishman got up, too, and led the way around the tree to the place where he had set his traveling forge in the shade beside a spring.

All the tools Sequoyah had seen the Englishman use were small, for the tinker had to carry them in his saddle packs. The forge was a cube of cold iron, or steel, as the tinker called it. The goatskin bellows weren't much larger than a lady's fan, and the brass tube through which they puffed air at the fire was no bigger around than the clay stem of Sequoyah's pipe. The hammers and forceps and pliers that the tinker used were in sizes to fit with the smallness of the forge and the bellows, but they were made of the best of metal, and he could work wonders with them, as Sequoyah had seen.

But now the Englishman opened another saddle pack, which, earlier, he had laid off to one side on the ground, and took out tools that were even smaller and finer than those he used to mend pots. He laid these out on the ground beside the forge, blew up his fire with his bellows, and took the silver shilling in the grip of his tongs. He held the coin over the flame, turning it this way and that, till the metal began to soften and the engraving began to blur. Then he laid the shilling on the forge and pounded at it with one of his smallest hammers.

The coin spread. It was no longer a circle, but an oval. The blurred design—King George's head—disappeared from the surface as King George's power had disappeared from the United States. Again the tinker heated the coin, and again he pounded it. Working steadily, humming endlessly under his breath about the wee cooper o' Fife, he turned the shilling into a ribbon of metal thinner than any metal object Sequoyah had ever seen, pliable enough to bend on itself till it doubled, and still strong enough not to break.

61

"Give me your hand," said the tinker at last, and Sequoyah held out his hand. The tinker bent the ribbon of metal around the Indian boy's wrist, a white-metal bracelet that weighed so little he hardly knew it was there.

"Now," said his teacher, laughing, "when you can do as well, boy, you will be a silversmith."

Before Sequoyah was over the wonder of metal that could be worked thinner than cloth, the Englishman had loaded up his ponies and was gone.

After that day Sequoyah began to get the name of being a hard trader.

"He's taking after his father," people said, but they said it behind his back. No one dared remind him to his face that he was not all Cherokee.

He wanted silver, any kind of silver. He refused to be paid in bushels of corn, or in deerskins, or even in woodpecker feathers and freshwater pearls. Silver he wanted and silver he must have, although he would take copper coins when they were offered. He figured that he could trade them for silver later.

Silver bracelets, silver buckles and buttons, silver earrings, silver knife handles—once, even, a silver snuffbox for John Ross. Spoons and forks of silver. When he had no silver he went back to working with iron and copper, but silver was his love and his great joy. He learned not only to heat and pound it, but to work designs on the surfaces of spoons and forks and ornaments with a graving tool. He learned to rub the silver with wood ash and a piece of buckskin until it glowed. And he made his own mark, a tiny thing, almost invisible, to scratch on the under surface of each piece he made, like Paul Revere and the other silversmiths John Ross told of, away to the north.

Sequoyah did not grow rich after he became a silversmith. There were few people anywhere in the Cherokee Nation who were rich in money. People counted their wealth in acres of land and bushels of crops harvested; in food stored for winter, and well-filled barns. Sequoyah was contented with a roof over his head and enough to fill him. A horse was good, for he could load a horse with his tools and travel from place to place as the notion struck him. He often went back into the Overhill country to work for the people there, and when they paid him in garden truck or clothing he turned what he took in over to his mother. But he went back to the Valley towns again and again, for in the Valley towns he could trade his work for silver.

Life in the United States was changing faster in those days than it had when the same country used to be a group of English colonies. There were many reasons why the rate of change had speeded up.

In the first place, of course, the new country had been established by young men who were trying out an almost-new system of government. They were experimenting with their lives and fortunes as physicists in laboratories today experiment with atomic power. These physicists of government were not always sure what would come out of the test tubes into which they had stirred courage, determination, and blind faith in about equal parts. Sometimes the results proved highly explosive.

All the world was bubbling with the same kind of excitement. Much of the earth's surface had been explored by Sequoyah's time. The outlines of the continents had been mapped, although what lay within the ocean boundaries of the land forms was still largely unknown. But men began to feel that they had conquered their

64

physical world, and they turned to the conquest of the elements. They began to experiment with steam, first as a means of navigation and later for propelling land transports.

Europe's governments were bubbling experimentally, too. The French were trying new forms of self-government, and whatever happened in France was bound to affect England and Germany and Italy and Russia almost as much at it did France itself. Emigrants left Europe and sailed to the New World to help settle the new United States. With them the newcomers brought all kinds of ideas, ideas about work and teaching and new uses of raw materials. The land to which they came was a great one. No one yet knew its exact area, or what trees and plains and mountains and rivers covered its surface. For the time being, there was land enough and to spare, to be had for the taking. Indians—red savages, noble, perhaps, but savages all the same—lived upon it, but they made no use of it in the sense that a white man would. It was a shame, said Europe's landless, that this good land should be wasted. They followed the trails to the back of beyond, and if the Indians objected they let them object.

Few of the white people already living in the United States realized what changes were being brought to them from overseas, for the changes came gradually, a few at a time. Even fewer of the Indians could perceive what was happening. Even men like John Ross, educated in the north in the cities along the coast, hardly comprehended that their lands were being infiltrated until it was too late. Probably one who lived quietly, away from the roads and the movement of peoples along them, as Sequoyah did, saw the changes even less clearly.

But as time went on, even such a quiet, remote section of the United States as the Cherokee country was affected by the changes that went on along the Atlantic seaboard and spread inland along the rivers. In one way, the changes were felt comparatively early in the Cherokee country because the Cherokees had allied themselves with the British in the Revolutionary War. They were under suspicion by the American citizens of the new, neighboring states. Particularly were they suspected of possible treachery by the Georgians, who were convinced that no Cherokee ever could or should be trusted.

There were missions and schools in the Cherokee country, as we have said. The missionaries were hopeful of drawing more and more children to them, of teaching them to read and write, of training them in the ways of Christianity. They firmly believed that the children would, in time, teach and convert their parents. But sometimes the most devout missionaries gave way to discouragement. The children seemed to learn more slowly than white children of the same age, and, if the children learned slowly, how much more slowly would their parents learn than white adults. At such times the missionaries seem to have overlooked the fact that the Indian children had to learn to speak and understand the English language before they could use it as a tool in reading and writing.

All around the Cherokee Nation, the new United States needed businesses and businessmen in order to develop properly. More and more traders' licenses were granted by the government to men who wanted to go into or through the Indian country. The lands the Indians occupied were guaranteed to them by treaties. The first treaties had been made with Great Britain, but at the end of the Revolution a whole new set of treaties was made with the

United States government, to protect the Indians' lives and lands.

According to the treaties, no white men could live in the Cherokee Nation without specific permission from its chief and governing council. But nothing had been written down to close the Cherokee roads to white travelers. And the roads that led through the Cherokee Nation went from Virginia and West Virginia into the Carolinas, Georgia, and Mississippi, and on—through the French colony of Louisiana to its capital city, New Orleans. The roads and the rivers of the Nation became main thoroughfares, ever more heavily traveled.

After ten years of the life of the United States, any Cherokee who wanted to remain a Cherokee was aware that his country was in danger from the encroaching white men. Any Cherokee who wanted to marry and raise a family was bound to worry a lot about what was going to happen to him and to his Nation. Sequoyah had much on his mind in the years when a new country and a new century were growing together, all around him.

When Sequoyah was about nineteen years old, he married a girl from a Valley town. He was too closely related to the people in the Overhill country to look for a wife there. He was afraid he might fall in love with a girl and then discover, as one of his cousins had, that she was a member of his own clan. That made her legally his sister. Sequoyah's cousin never married—he lived and died a bachelor—for the girl he wanted was one he must not have. Sequoyah did not want that to happen to him.

Besides, most of his work was in the lowlands. He had heard tales of white men who married women from other parts of the country, and who had to give up work to take their wives back to the places they came from. His own mother had refused to leave her homeland when she married. After all, Sequoyah never tried to deny to himself that he was half white and that what happened to white men could possibly happen to him. All in all, he thought it was better for him to marry a girl from one of the Valley towns.

But he did marry a girl who was a Cherokee full-blood. That much he could do. And theirs was a thoroughly Cherokee home. They had a one-room log cabin with a fireplace built against one inside end wall. The chimney was made by lacing willow and dogwood sticks together

Sequoyah and his wife had a thoroughly Cherokee home

around upright poles. Then the basketwork frame was thickly coated with mud, and as the first mud dried, more was smeared on. "Wattle and daub," they called such chimneys, which were made like the walls of Indian houses before the white men came. It was a way of building that spread from the Maya country in Mexico as far northward as the Ohio valley. And, curi-

70

ously, it was an old way of building in Europe, too. The houses of peasants in France and Italy and Spain were sometimes of wattle-and-daub construction.

There were no windows in that first cabin— Sequoyah would not have glass on his place. The door was hung on heavy rawhide hinge straps, and most of the year it stood open to admit both light and air to the interior of the house. On days when the weather was wet or cold and the door had to be closed, the firelight from the hearth brightened the room. The floor was made of earth, pounded hard and swept smooth.

Sequoyah built a bunk bed along the wall at the other end of the room, facing the fireplace, and he made a table and four wooden stools, which together almost filled the middle of the room. There were shelves on the long wall facing the door, and his wife's tall walnut spinning wheel stood in the corner between the fireplace and the door. On the other side of the fireplace, against the inner wall, was a cradle in which Sequoyah's wife had been rocked when she was a baby. It had been a long time since Cherokee women had put their babies to bed in blanket hammocks hung from the house rafters. Sequo-

71

yah could not argue his wife out of using a white woman's hooded cradle with rockers.

There was a snake-and-rider fence around the door lot, and inside it a flower and herb garden grew. Here they planted morning-glories and the kind of moss roses that have haws as big as crab apples, and feverfew and tansy, and lavender and marjoram. There were wattle-and-daub beehives against the fence, for the honey was useful for cooking and wax brought a good price from the traders, who sold it again to the candlemakers. Sequoyah's wife hung empty gourds, with small round doors cut in them, from the branches of the trees, so that the martins would nest near the house.

In the shade of a walnut tree down by the creek, on the edge of the spring pool where water cress thrived, four kinds of wild mint flourished. And spreading out beyond the fenced door lot were the vegetable garden and the field where Sequoyah planted his corn, with the squash vines running between the rows and binding the cornstalks together.

There was no paint on the cabin—Sequoyah would not even have whitewash. Even so, Indian life had become so much like white life in that area that it would have been hard for a traveler to tell the skin color of the family that lived in the cabin, unless he happened to see someone outside the house, working in the yard. The hides that were pegged up to dry against the outside walls would tell him nothing. Indians and whites alike used slabs of native white limestone for doorsteps. Chimneys and hand-riven shingles were the same. A white woman, just as well as an Indian, could have pounded her corn meal in the hollowed tree trunk that stood on end beside the door. Still, if you had asked Sequoyah, he would have told you—and honestly insisted—that he and his wife were Indian, and that the way they lived was entirely the Cherokee way.

4

The Talking Leaves

To use an old southern expression, Sequoyah and his wife rocked along for several years after they were married. They were neither rich nor poor, but comfortably in the middle. A craftsman who was also a farmer could support his family well in those days. People said that you would hardly know that Sequoyah was half white; he took care of his wife and his growing family just as any Cherokee would.

74

One idea that is so interesting it could almost be made into a kind of game is guessing what would have happened to certain famous people if they had been born in other times or other surroundings than their own. If, for example, Sequoyah had been born three hundred years earlier, in Mexico, he would probably have been one of the Maya priests who left us the paintings, done with earth colors on deer hide and maguey paper, that give us such knowledge as we have of their people and the way in which they lived and worshiped.

But Sequoyah was born in 1775, the year of American independence, and thirty-seven years later, when the War of 1812 broke out, he was a grown man with a family and a business and many responsibilities. Yet—what would have happened if he hadn't gone to war?

Actually, the Cherokees took part in the War of 1812 because it gave them a chance to settle a grudge of their own. Traditionally, the Cherokees were enemies of the tribes of the Creek Confederacy, who lived to the south of the Cherokee country. As long as the Indians were left alone, the enmity was not too serious. But as time passed and the white invaders pressed in

75

on the tribes from three sides, Indian lands became more and more precious. Boundaries were
more sharply drawn, and each tribe learned from
the whites that land itself was something to be
clutched, not shared. Therefore, the Cherokees
and the Creeks fought ever more bitterly over
the boundaries between their territories.

If the Creeks had not first allied themselves
with the English, the Cherokees certainly would
never have sided with the United States. All Indians had, in the past, received better treatment
and fairer trade from the English colonial offi-
cials than they now did from the government of
the new states. But because the Creeks were the
allies of the English and the Cherokees had often
before fought against the Creeks, the Cherokees
found themselves enlisting as border troops under General Andrew Jackson. Many of them
hoped that if the Americans were victorious one
result of the alliance would be new, and better,
treaties with the Nation.

At first Sequoyah did not pay much attention
to the war and the rumors of the war. He was
busy at home in his garden, or at the forge when
people brought him work to do. He paid far less

attention to the war talk, as a matter of fact, than he did to the discussions of some of his friends who wanted to leave Tennessee for good and settle in Mexico.

Back in 1782, when Sequoyah himself was only seven years old, the first Cherokee group to leave the country had applied to the Spanish governor of Louisiana for permission to settle in New Spain. Permission had been granted to them, and lands had been set aside and guaranteed for the use of the Cherokees in the western part of what is now the state of Arkansas. Ever since, a few Cherokees at a time had loaded their goods on flatboats, floated down the Holston River to the Tennessee, down the Tennessee to the Mississippi, and down the Mississippi to the mouth of the Arkansas. Then they had struggled upstream to about the place where Fort Smith, Arkansas, now stands. There was a good-sized Indian community there in 1803, when the United States purchased Louisiana, and Arkansas ceased to be a part of a foreign possession.

By 1808 the western Cherokees were calling themselves the Nation West and inviting the people of the Nation East to join them in their new, free country. They had made treaties with the United States government, and felt secure in the protection those treaties promised them.

One of the Raincrow cousins persuaded Sequoyah to go to the wars. He came riding up to the gate in the yard fence late one afternoon, with his musket slung over one shoulder and a bow and arrows over the other. Sequoyah was sitting on the doorstep with his youngest child in his lap. This one was a girl, the first girl after four boys. She was fat and sassy, crowing out loud and pretending to struggle free of her father's arms. When she saw the horse she stretched out her fat little brown hands toward it.

"My cousin," Sequoyah said. He tucked the baby under one arm and limped down to the gate, swinging it open with his free hand. "Get down and come in."

"Thank you," his cousin answered, "I will."

Sequoyah turned his head toward the house and called his oldest boy.

"Tessee," he said, "come and take our cousin's horse."

The boy came, quickly and willingly.

"Take him around to the shed and unsaddle," Sequoyah directed. He turned back to his cousin.

"Come in and sit down," he invited him. "My wife will have food ready presently."

"Thank you," his cousin repeated. The two men walked together to the door of the house. Sequoyah's wife was waiting to meet their guest. She laid her palm gently against his for a moment, and then held out her arms to her husband for the baby. Sequoyah shook his head.

"I'll keep her," he said. "She won't bother us, and you'll be busy."

The two men dropped down on the doorstep. Tessee came around the corner of the house and handed his cousin a gourd dipper dripping with fresh cold water from the spring. There was a pause, while the cousin rested and Sequoyah and Tessee waited. When the time came, when the visitor was ready, he would tell the family why he was there and why he came armed. Asking questions before he spoke would be a rude thing for a Cherokee to do.

"I'm going south," he said, when he was ready to speak.

"How far?" Sequoyah asked. Questions were all right now. His cousin had suggested what he wanted to talk about.

"To join the troops."

79

"Across the line into Georgia?"

"Yes. And on south as far as need be."

Sequoyah shook his head thoughtfully. "They don't like Indians in Georgia. They don't like any Indians, but especially they don't like us Cherokees."

"I know that," his cousin said.

There was a rustle of cloth behind them, and Sequoyah's wife stood in the doorway. "Supper is ready," she said, and the two men rose and followed her into the house. Sequoyah laid the baby in her cradle, and Tessee took a piece of corn bread from the wooden bowl at his mother's place and gave it to the little sister to chew on. The rest of them sat in silence on their puncheon stools while Sequoyah asked the Powers Above to bless their food.

When they had finished their corn bread and beans and venison stew, Sequoyah lighted his pipe and turned to his cousin again.

"Cherokees are safer if they keep out of Georgia," he said, as if they had never interrupted their words.

"I know that," his cousin answered. "But I think this, Sequoyah. If the Cherokees are to make a good treaty with the United States—

80

better than any we have been able to make so far—they will have to make friends with the Americans first. And I believe that if we fight *with* the Americans and *against* the Creeks and the English, we will be able to persuade the Americans that we are friendly and that they should help us."

"Yes, the Creeks are fighting on the side of the English," Sequoyah agreed.

"I know it," his cousin answered. He did not say, *Your father was an Englishman. No one will blame you if you stay at home, or even if you say you are friendly to the English.*

"I will go with you," Sequoyah decided. He did not say, *My father was English. Therefore I must fight all Englishmen.* Without any other words, he showed his cousin where to unroll his blanket on the floor. And still without wasting speech he rose in the morning and prepared to ride with his Raincrow kinsman. He kissed the baby's round, soft cheek, and he laid his hand for a moment first on Tessee's shoulder and then on his wife's, before he caught each of the younger boys in turn in his arms. He took the roll of blankets and the bag of meal his wife handed him, and lifted his musket down from its pegs above the fireplace. Then he was ready, and he went out of the house and hauled himself into the saddle Tessee had put on the back of the mouse-gray pony.

The Cherokees fought, and fought well, during the War of 1812. The war ended, as far as their campaign against the Creeks was concerned, in the Battle of Horseshoe Bend on the Tallapoosa River in Georgia. It was the twenty-seventh of March, 1814. Some of the Cherokees went on south, following General Jackson, after it was over, but most of them, like Sequoyah, were tired. They had done what they set out to do: they had licked the Creeks. It was the end of March, which meant that it was already late in the year to start planting their gardens. But there was still time to make some sort of crop, and they gathered in groups of twos and threes, each cluster made up of men who came from the same town or neighborhood, and started along the road for home.

Thinking things over as the gray pony jogged along to the northward, Sequoyah was discouraged at first. He had been gone from home for

82

two years. The children would have grown so much that he wouldn't know them when he saw them. Tessee must have been the man of the family—after all, the boy was fourteen when his father left—unless Tessee had taken it into his head to go out fighting too. That could have happened without Sequoyah's knowing a thing about it. For there had not been one man who

Sequoyah went forth to fight in the War of 1812

came into camp after he did who hailed from his own part of the country and so could bring him news.

Of course, the baby would be unrecognizable. She had been just standing up, holding onto his finger, when he left. Why, by now, two years later, she was walking. Walking! She was certainly talking, too; they said girls always began to talk earlier than boys, and Tessee was jabbering a streak before he was two. What, Sequoyah wondered, had been the first word his baby girl had said?

His thoughts took another, related, turn. He remembered how the white soldiers had got news from home when they were in the Army. They had not had to wait for men from their home towns to join up and be assigned to the units in which they served. No, those white men got news direct, on sheets of paper that looked like the dry, withered leaves of strange trees. A man would think those leaves could talk; the signs that were drawn on them told the white men so much.

And then, the white soldiers could, in turn, send word to their own families. Any man who knew how could take a goose quill and a bottle of ink made by boiling oak galls and iron filings together in spring water, and make those talking tracks on a piece of paper. Some of them, who had no paper, used thin corn husks or pieces of hide or bark or even sycamore leaves.

Not every white man knew how to make the leaves talk, he remembered. He would see groups of soldiers gathered around one who could write, telling him what messages to put down so they could send word home to their families. And he could remember the ones who could not read bringing their letters to those who could. They would listen to the reading of the messages on the paper over and over, sometimes, until they memorized every word.

That was it, he figured out. The marks were sounds; the marks stood for sounds. A word was a sound, too. Then a mark and a word were the same sound, when you knew how to recognize one by the other. Make a mark, and if you knew the sound it represented, you knew the word, too. It was that easy.

Why hadn't Indians figured it all out long ago? Indians were as smart as white men any day.

The white soldiers got their news on sheets of paper

If the whites could read and write, the Indians could learn to do so. Perhaps someday they would. He jogged on through the woods toward home, the thought rolling around in his mind.

5

Lost Work

Now Sequoyah found himself in a situation many other war veterans have had to go through. He had had sense enough to know that everything would be slightly changed when he got home. At the same time, humanly and foolishly, he had hoped that nothing would have changed at all. Most of all, it had never entered his head to expect changes in himself. *He* was the same person, *he* was the identical Sequoyah who had gone away. *He* had lived with himself all those days, and he knew he was the same. But without changing his skin, or even consciously changing his mind, his outlook on many things had altered so completely that he was actually a very different person from the man who had left his home to go to the wars with Cousin Raincrow.

The biggest change he found at home, of course, was in the children. Tessee was a young man—a good farmer and a hard worker who went through the day from dawn to dusk without saying more than a dozen words. He had kept the family together while his father was gone, with a roof over their heads and food in their mouths, but he had little to tell of how he had done so.

However, when Sequoyah first drew rein at the gate in the yard fence, Tessee was out in the field, and the other boys were working with him, so their father did not see them. Instead, he saw a little girl, in a gray linsey-woolsey dress, playing busily by the door. She had her doll perched opposite her on the doorstep, and she was having a party, with hollyhocks for teacups and their broad, flat green leaves for saucers. When she saw the man at the gate, she could not remember him to recognize him. But she stopped playing

89

to watch him for a moment, and then ran down the path to the gate, bringing her doll along behind her by one arm.

"You come in," she said like a grown woman, still clutching the doll's hand as if it were a child's. Sequoyah laughed as he dropped from the horse's back and tied the reins around the gatepost before he opened the gate. The little girl held the doll out toward him. "Here," she said. "You take her."

Sequoyah threw back his head and laughed, and his wife, hearing the sound, came and stood in the door, facing him. He picked the little girl and the doll up in his arms, and started toward the house. "Look!" he said excitedly. "She brought it right to me! That must be her name. Ah-yoka. She Brought It."

"It's a good name," his wife replied. "It's a lucky name. The first name her father gives her when he comes home from fighting ought to be a good one for her whole life long. Come in. Come in, and be welcome in your home."

She cooked a huge supper that night, and when Tessee and the other boys came in from the fields, they could only stand and stare and stare at the father who had come back to them.

90

The family was together again, and that first
night was a very good and happy one for all of
them.

Sequoyah slept late the next morning, and
when he wakened the house was quiet except
for the small snaps of the flames in the fireplace
biting at a fresh piece of log, and the rising and
falling cry, half-hum, half-wail, of his wife's
spinning wheel. He rolled over in his bunk bed

Sequoyah's first night home was a happy one for all

and looked at his wife, who was stepping back and drawing her arm down behind her, bowing to the tall wheel, and then moving forward and raising her hand to greet the spindle, it seemed, as she wound up the thread she had just drawn from the carded wool.

"How quiet it all is!" Sequoyah said. "Where are the children?"

"The boys have gone to the fields," his wife answered him, "and your daughter is playing house on the doorstep. Are you ready for breakfast?"

He got up and went outdoors to wash at the spring; then he came back to the house and sat down on the doorstep with the bowl of yellow corn-meal mush his wife handed him. Ordinarily, at home, he would have gone to the fields with the boys, hours and hours earlier, or he would have been shoeing a horse or beating out a knife blade or a bracelet for a neighbor. But the boys had gone to work without him and the neighbors didn't know he was at home.

He ate the mush slowly, enjoying every bite, and when he had finished he set the bowl behind him, blindly, with one hand. He idled there in the warm sun, listening to the lonesome rise and fall of the spinning behind him, to his wife's footsteps moving in time to the wheel's song as if she were dancing to it. He watched his daughter setting hollyhock cups on leaf saucers. Ah-yoka looked at her father and smiled, and he remembered how he used to amuse the boys when they were her age. He held out his hand to his daughter and smiled back at her.

"Bring me one of your leaves, and a rose thorn, and I'll draw a picture for you," he said.

This was a new game to Ah-yoka. She obeyed willingly. She brought a fresh, flat hollyhock leaf and the longest and sharpest thorn she could find. Then she snuggled against her father and watched while he flattened the leaf on his knee and began to draw a picture with the thorn.

"Here is the house," he showed her, "and here is the gate. Shall we make the path to join them?"

"Yes!" Ah-yoka said, eagerly.

"Here's the path, then. Now, here are the hollyhocks—you'll have to get me another thorn, little one. I broke the point of this one on the vein of the leaf—thank you. *Here* are the hollyhocks, and here are the roses——"

"Draw a horse!"

"Please?"

To amuse Ah-yoka he drew pictures on hollyhock leaves

"Please."

It was no different from what he had done hundreds of times before to amuse the boys. It was no different from drawing designs on silver before he cut them deeper with a graving point. It was all thoroughly familiar, this having a point in one hand and a leaf in the other. Surely, if he went on with this familiar occupation, the hollyhock leaf could be made to talk.

He threw it away from him impatiently, and his hands felt strangely empty.

"Let's go down to the creek," he said to Ah-yoka. "Maybe we can find a piece of sycamore bark to draw pictures on."

As long as they were down there, wandering along in the cool pleasantness of shade, Sequoyah and Ah-yoka gathered all the white, smooth pieces of bark that they could carry. When they came back to the house, the mother met them at the door.

"Lunch is ready," she said, and led them indoors to the table.

After lunch Sequoyah went back to his seat on the doorstep. The sun had slipped around to the other side of the house and the doorstep was shaded now, but the day was warmer than it had been in the morning, and so the shade was welcome. Sequoyah laid his pile of bark beside him and considered it. Then he hoisted himself up again and went back to the fireplace for a piece of hard hickory charcoal to use for drawing.

"Draw me," Ah-yoka commanded.

"Ah-yoka," said her father. "Ah-yoka. She Brought It. Ah. Well. This is Ah, this mark

95

here. And this is yoka. Yoka. Put them together and they are Ah-yoka. That is your picture of you, little one."

"It doesn't look much like me," his critic observed.

"No, it doesn't look like you. But it sounds like you. And now I am drawing pictures of sounds."

"Draw another one. Draw a picture of you."

"Se-quoy-ah. Se-quoy-ah. Let's see. The last sound of my name is the first sound of yours. That's easy. I can put the Ah sound down at the end of my name. Now I need two other signs——"

"That doesn't look like you, either."

He sat and thought awhile. Maybe drawing signs for sounds was wrong. Perhaps there should be a sign for a word. Ah-yoka might be right. A drawing of a little girl would mean Ah-yoka. But would that mean just his one little girl, this Ah-yoka here before him, or any little girl at all, or all little girls everywhere? And then, her name, Ah-yoka, did not mean a little girl, except in this one family. It meant She Brought It, and that was very different. It was a different idea. Should a drawing of a little

96

girl stand for the idea of bringing? That thought seemed too complicated to Sequoyah to worry with at all.

He would try his own name, then. Sequoyah, The Lame One. That was easier. It was one idea and one only, a limping man. He sketched a kind of stick figure on the bark, and to show what he meant he drew it with one leg shorter than the other, and a cane in the opposite hand

"Is that you, Daddy?"

"That's me—*I*, I mean. That's a lame man, and it stands for me. Can you remember it?"

"I guess." But Ah-yoka was only three, and she was getting tired of this game. She turned her back on her father and returned to playing house with hollyhocks. But now she had some plain leaf plates and some leaf plates with designs on them, like the four blue-and-white plates her mother had bought from the trader and ever since had kept on the top shelf of the cupboard.

Sequoyah was still at it when the boys came home; still drawing on his pieces of bark when his wife called them all to supper. When the meal was finished, Sequoyah sat by the fireplace and used the light from the burning logs for scratching more and more signs on the curled bits of sycamore bark.

This was the biggest change in Sequoyah when he came home from the wars. He had lost interest in the jobs that used to engage him. The boys could do the work of the fields and his wife could keep up the house and her spinning. Ah-yoka could play beside him, and stop her play to talk to him, and return to her games, without his seeming to notice. Sequoyah sat with his sticks of charcoal and his bits of bark, mouthing words over and over, scratching marks on the white wood, and letting the world go by.

He was always glad to see people. Anyone who came to the gate could have his attention. He would hail the person and invite him in, and give him a seat—on the doorstep when the weather was warm and sunny, by the fire when it was rainy or cold. After the first greetings, Sequoyah's words never varied.

"Give me a word," he would say to the newcomer. When he had the word, he would do one of two things. Either he would sit mouthing it, with his eyes half closed while he spoke the word over and over, then opening them suddenly when the idea behind the word came to him and he began to draw on his piece of bark. Or he would repeat the word, more slowly, then pick up a pile of bark slabs and turn over every one, looking, looking, to recognize the sign he had drawn before for the same word. Sometimes the word was so familiar he identified it easily; sometimes it was less usual, and he had to give up the search and start drawing a new sign for that idea.

There were thousands of words in the Cherokee language, and of course every word had at least one idea behind it. The astonishing thing was that Sequoyah could recognize as many of his idea pictures as he could. He realized that it would take him years and years to make drawings for all those thousands of words. What was the difference? If the Cherokees could ever write their ideas, they could record their history and religion; they could send letters across long distances to one another; they would be a people as powerful as any whites, for their minds would be as powerful as the white men's minds, and their records would be as complete. It never occurred to Sequoyah to wonder if he thought of writing in this way—as the most important single

99

thing in the world—partly because his own father had been a white man.

There was a windstorm one night, howling around the house and ripping at the shakes of the roof with sharp sleet fingers. Half asleep, Sequoyah was conscious of wet cold driving at his face. He pulled the blanket over his head and slept on.

"The roof is half gone," his wife told him in the morning.

"Is it?" he asked. "That reminds me—I haven't a sign for roof. How did I happen to overlook that one?" He reached for a piece of charcoal, but his wife came and planted herself, with her skirts spread, between him and the pile of charred hickory sticks he now kept always within reach.

"The roof needs mending," she insisted, raising her voice.

"Tessee can do it——"

"Tessee can *not* do it. Tessee cannot do all the work in the fields, and take odd jobs around the neighborhood to support us all, and come home to mend the roof. *You* can do it."

"All right," said Sequoyah peaceably. He finished his breakfast and pushed the mush bowl back on the table. "I'll fix it."

His wife picked up the bowl and went to scrub it clean with wet sand, by the doorstep. She was gone five minutes, and when she came back Sequoyah had a piece of bark on the table before him, and was drawing on it busily.

"I thought you were going to fix the roof."

"I *am* going to fix the roof."

"When?"

"Right away. In just a minute. As soon as I get these signs for 'roof' and 'shake' down so I won't forget——"

There was the rush of a long gray skirt past him, and the wind of his wife's movement blew half the pieces of bark off the table. She scooped up the rest—in her hands, in her arms, any way at all so she got hold of them. With one sweep she flung the slabs that were Sequoyah's two years' work into the heart of the fire.

"Now!" she said, pointing to the door. "Go out there and draw your signs for 'shake' and 'roof.' Draw them on top of this house, before we are all out in the cold for the rest of our lives."

Sequoyah rose, very slowly, and stood and

101

She flung two years' work into the heart of the fire

looked at her. "You burned them," he said. "You burned every one of them."

"Not every one," snapped his wife. "Not yet, but I will now." She dashed about the room, laying hands on sheets of bark, skimming them sidewise across the floor into the fire. Her husband watched her, still without moving, without speaking to her again.

"Go on!" she screamed. "Go on! Go on out and fix the roof! Don't drive poor Tessee to do everything! You used to be a good man—before you went crazy over your signs and pieces of rubbish. What's happened to you? Don't you care about anything else in the world any more?"

Ah-yoka huddled in a corner, watching and listening. Her whole little body shook with fear, for she had never seen her mother angry before, but she was as quiet as her father. Sequoyah turned from his wife and crossed the room to the little girl. He gathered her into his arms and stood facing the furious woman, the child's face pressed against his shoulder.

"I care about her," he said. "Be quiet. You're frightening her."

"I won't be quiet!" his wife stormed. "I've been quiet long enough—as long as I'm going to

103

be quiet. I used to have a good Cherokee husband. Now I'm married to a worthless white man. Get out of this house!"

"Yes," said Sequoyah almost in a whisper. He crossed to the bunk and picked up two blankets. He wrapped one around Ah-yoka, and the other he flung across his own shoulder. "Good-bye," he said. "We're getting out." And he shut the door very quietly behind them and carried Ah-yoka down the path to the gate without either of them once looking back.

6
The Leaves Talk to the Cherokees

There was an old cabin away in the woods, midway between the Valley towns and those of the Uplands. The old couple who had built the cabin and lived in it until just before the Creek War broke out, were dead. They had been distant cousins of Wut-teh's; therefore, Sequoyah thought, he was one of their kinfolks and had as good a right as anybody to occupy what was left of their house. His wife had called him a white man; he was in truth half white, and like any other white man, he told himself, he would squat on Indian lands.

He grinned a little, one side of his mouth twisting up, when he saw that the roof of this cabin, too, had fallen in. There was no getting away from a roof repair job. Diligently he set to work, and within a week he had his roof weather-tight, alternating bark slabs with old shakes that had blown off onto the ground. There were two small glass windows in one wall, miraculously unbroken, and the fireplace in the long wall facing the door would still draw. Sequoyah left the window lights in place. He would need all the light he could get to work by, and who minded glass windows in a white man's cabin?

He and Ah-yoka did not live like white people, however. Sequoyah hunted with bow and arrows (for he had left his gun behind when he rushed out of his wife's house) and brought in game for their meat. It was too late in the year to put in a garden at the new place, but he traded deer hides and meat to his neighbors, who lived a mile away downhill, for corn meal and dried beans and squash and a jug of molasses. He dried some of his meat and brought in firewood and generally got ready for winter. Wherever he went, through the woods or along the trails, he gathered smooth pieces of bark and long, slender, hardwood poles that he could burn slowly to make charcoal pencils.

He thought a great deal on those long, wandering walks. They traveled slowly in the underbrush, the little girl and her lame father, looking around them at the wonders of the world, in the forms of leaf and light, that the wood spirits had laid out to delight human beings who would take time to see. Sometimes Sequoyah thought he saw movements among the leaves without bodily cause for the stirring, and he never failed to show the glimmer of light and motion to Ahyoka.

"Look, little one. The Wood Spirits—The Little People from Under the Ground—the people who are even smaller than you—are running before us. If we are very quiet, and rest, perhaps they will come back."

But however long they sat, however still they sat, they never saw The Little People from Under the Ground, although now and then they were sure they heard tiny, unearthly, twittering voices far in the distance.

107

The Little People had helped and protected the Cherokees on their long journeys and through their long history. It could have been they who came to Sequoyah's aid now, and who turned his thoughts back to his first attempts to make signs for words. He remembered that the first syllable of Ah-yoka's name and the last syllable of his own were the same. Once he had thought of drawing a single sign for the two. Perhaps he had been on the right trail then. Perhaps he should make signs for sounds, as he had originally thought, instead of signs for words.

"Little one," he said to Ah-yoka, "make a noise."

"What noise, Daddy?"

"That's a good one. Wha. How do you make it?"

"You put your mouth almost shut and whistle. Like this. Wha."

"There really are two sounds there, not one. The whistle sound and the ah sound. Perhaps that noise would need two signs."

"Maybe," said Ah-yoka blithely. She never entirely understood what he was talking about, but since he never talked about anything else—

he just went ahead and *did* other things—she was sure that whatever it was, it was important.

Then, on a day when they were going through the woods looking for bloodroot to dry and store for medicine in case either of them had a stomach ache, they crossed the main trail, a few miles above the mission school. They had crossed the trail many times before, and they naturally paused to look along it, to see if any of their neighbors were traveling from one place to another, when they came to the wide road.

Ah-yoka thought at first she saw a stone lying on the trail. "Look, Daddy, what a funny stone," she said, and then insisted, "Look! It's a funny shape!"

Sequoyah turned his eyes to follow her pointing finger. For a moment he studied the object she indicated, carefully. "I don't believe that's a stone," he said then, and led the way the short distance along the trail to find out what it was his daughter had discovered.

It lay in his palm when he had grasped it and straightened up—a small, compact, blue-bound volume. The letters on its spine and front read, *First School Speller,* but Sequoyah did not know

109

that. All he knew was that he held, in his own palm, a collection of the talking leaves, bunched and sewn together, and given a tight smooth cover to keep them clean. He fluttered the pages forward and back. Signs were there on the leaves, many signs, each one often repeated. A white man's collection of signs, put into his hands when he most needed it.

"Little one," he said to Ah-yoka, almost in a whisper, "this does not belong to us, and we do not know whose it is. But we are going to take it home with us, and keep it safe there. If we ever find the owner we will return it to him, but in the meantime he surely will not mind if we look at it."

"We can wash our hands first," said Ah-yoka. Her father was just beginning to teach her how important hand-washing was.

"We can wash our hands before we look at it, and we can keep it wrapped in a piece of deer hide, safely, when we are not using it," Sequoyah agreed. He thrust the book into his shirt front. "Come on, Ah-yoka, let's go home. We can look for bloodroot again some other day."

As time went on, and he studied the book, Sequoyah saw how important sounds were—must be—in all languages. He copied the signs from the speller, and fitted them to sounds of his own, for it seemed sensible to use signs people had already agreed on as much as possible. But there were really only twenty-six signs in the book, used over and over again, as he soon discovered. He used most of them, some of them drawn in the white man's way and others turned on their sides or upside down because he thought they were handsomer like that. When the white man's signs had all received Cherokee sounds, he began adding signs of his own again.

That winter, when it was hard to get through the woods—although the deer were easier to find and to bring down when he did go—Sequoyah spent almost all his time working on the sounds and signs. At first he thought there were thousands of sounds in Cherokee, almost as many as there were words, even if the white men did get by with twenty-six scratches. For a while he piled up almost as many charcoal-marked pieces of bark as he had the first time. But as the winter wore on, and he and Ah-yoka sat and mouthed at one another, the number of signs grew smaller

111

and smaller. By the time spring came, he had reduced them from thousands to two hundred, and then reduced them further to just one hundred.

Now, in spring, Sequoyah began to add things up. It was time he took stock of himself. He was past forty. Word had come back to him from his old home that his wife was married again—and that the first thing her new husband had done was put a roof on the cabin and add a room for the boys to sleep in. Presumably his wife was happy enough. He hoped so. He and Ah-yoka had lived through the winter; they were both well and well fed, they had clothes on their backs and firewood in the pile. He himself had a trade —a craft—and he could support them both as well as he wanted to.

And here under his hand was his big secret, a hundred signs, each one standing for a Cherokee sound. When you put the signs together, in different combinations, you could make any words in the Cherokee language that you wanted to. He had tried the same signs for the few words he knew of Creek and Choctaw, and they seemed to work equally well for those languages. Here, under his hand, it seemed there was a way of

112

writing any Indian language he had ever heard of. Probably it was an equally satisfactory way of writing any language in the world.

He reflected that he had started out to make this way of writing for the benefit of the Cherokees. It might be of use and help to many more people than the members of his own tribe. But before he tried it—really tried out his system of sounds, even with his own people—Sequoyah wanted to make sure that it was *right*. The Cherokees of the Uplands did not speak exactly like the Cherokees of the Valleys, and neither group pronounced words just the same way as did the people who lived between them—the Middle Cherokees. He had to make sure his method would work for all three groups before he announced it to the Tribal Council. He was not yet quite ready to give away his secret.

He needed a chance to try out the system. He needed a place where he would be with people and could work with them, so he could make sure of what he was doing. It would help if he had members of all three Cherokee groups to work with. Some from each section of the old Cherokee Nation had gone across the Mississippi into Arkansas, where they had set up the Cherokee

113

Nation West. Why shouldn't he and Ah-yoka go out there and join them? The New Spain where the Indians had been given lands was gone, eaten up first by France and then by the United States. But the land was still there and the western Cherokees still lived on it. Why not take Ah-yoka and go and join them? There was nothing to hold him here in the Smoky Mountains.

All he really had to do was to put his quiver and bow case across his shoulders, sling his ax at his side, stuff his pipe in the tobacco pouch that hung from his belt, pick up the child, and set off downhill. Was that all, though? It was not. Above all else he had to take his pieces of bark with him, clumsy as they would be to carry. Then his eye fell on a rolled-up deerskin across the room. That was the answer. Copy the signs from the pieces of bark on the hide—in oak-gall-and-iron-filings ink they would not rub off—and then carry the skin across his shoulders, rolled in two blankets. The hide would be as light, and far more convenient to carry, as the scraps of bark.

So they set out again, Sequoyah carrying so little that it hardly seemed as if they could get along at all. He took the extra hides down the hill with him, and in the first settlement he traded them for a hammer, a pair of pliers, and a few scraps of metal—the minimum tinker's equipment. But with those few poor things he made their way, mending kettles and pots and putting handles on knives. Whenever he could, he took his pay in silver coins, and before long he had silver bracelets and earrings and half-moon-shaped neck gorgets to offer his customers. From then on, travel was easier.

They worked their way along on the flatboats, going down the smaller rivers to the larger ones and then on to the largest—the Mississippi. They went down the Mississippi on a great, heavily loaded timber float that was traveling to New Orleans.

They left the boat at the mouth of the Arkansas River, for now they were going to travel upstream, against the current, as flatboats could not go unless they were drawn by mule or ox teams. On a flat, sandy bar, at the mouth of the Arkansas River, Sequoyah and Ah-yoka fell in with another Cherokee family headed west.

There were a father and mother—two hardy, prosperous people—and their almost-grown sons and widowed daughter. Her husband, Sally told Sequoyah, had been killed in the Creek War,

115

and she and her eight-year-old son had lived with her parents ever since. No, she hadn't remarried. It wasn't that she had disliked marriage—quite the contrary. She had been very happy with her husband, and she didn't want to marry again until another man whom she could love and admire as much as her first husband came along.

Maybe it was the effect of spring in Arkansas. Arkansas springs are very specially beautiful. Maybe it was the two children—the boy of eight and the girl of almost seven—who played together so happily that it would have been a shame to separate them. Certainly the knowledge that he was doing the right thing, and that he was succeeding in work that was important to him, had made Sequoyah happier and more confident than he had felt for a long time. He and Sally were both lonesome people, starting out all over again in life in a new country, as if they had been ten or fifteen years younger than they actually were. Before they reached Fort Smith, they had decided to marry.

So Sequoyah was a married man, and a happily married man, when he took up his land and built his first cabin in the Cherokee Nation West. He and Sally did not stay very long in Fort Smith

116

or in nearby Polk County, where many Cherokees
had settled. They went on west and south, across
the Arkansas and Illinois rivers, into the low
hills where the town of Sallisaw, Oklahoma, is
now. There they built the log cabin that still
stands, inside a memorial building, and that you
can see if you visit Sallisaw.

Sequoyah made a joke about their going west
and south. "We're heading for Mexico," he told
Sally. "They say in the old people's legends that
once, centuries ago, the Cherokees lived there
and learned the most important things they know
today from the ancient Mexican people. So our
wisdom came from there, and here we are, going
back toward the source of our wisdom."

Sally brushed her fingers across his cheek as
lightly as a vine leaf fluttering across a sun path.
"You're a wise man yourself," she said. "Mexico
is the right place for you to go, if that's true."
They laughed together, at what they both
thought was a rather silly private joke.

Work in the new country was as hard as work
in a new country must always be. Ground had to
be cleared of trees and tangles of vines. Once,
working over a field on the second land terrace
above the river, Sequoyah discovered that what

117

he had cleared was not a little natural hill, as he had thought, but a mound of earth that had been constructed by men. Spread over the ground at its foot he found bits of chipped stone, among them a tiny arrowhead, and even, when he looked closely, fragments of painted pottery. He scooped up a handful of the things and carried them home to show to Sally and the children.

"Look," he said to them that evening, spreading his treasures out in the firelight, "people have been before us, even here."

Sally turned a piece of pottery over with a careful finger. "Indians," she commented. "Look. This is the sun design. They must have been Indians."

"Cherokees coming back from Mexico?" Sequoyah asked her lazily.

"Or Mexican Indians on the way down there," Sally answered, laughing. She gave her husband a little push. "Go on, get busy. It's time for the children's writing lesson."

Sequoyah laughed too, and turned to Ahyoka and The Squirrel Boy, her stepbrother. "Go and get your barks and charcoals," he instructed them. They all gathered in the firelight for that evening's lesson. Sally sat a little behind the chil-

118

dren and worked with them. But neither Sally nor Squirrel Boy learned as fast as little Ah-yoka. She was her father's daughter.

They had gone west in 1817. By 1821, what they thought of as a family game had become a real system of writing. Sequoyah would go out of the room, and Sally would dictate a message to one of the children.

"The beans are burning," Ah-yoka would write on a piece of bark; or, "The dog is baying at the foot of the tree," Squirrel Boy would scratch down. Then Sequoyah would return and read the sentence aloud. Next Ah-yoka would go out of the room while one of the others dictated. They took turn and turn about, all evening long, evening after evening. Sometimes they would make silly mistakes, half in fun, half to see if they really could trip each other up.

Then a time came when Sequoyah sent the children away to visit Sally's parents near Fort Smith. He made them each promise that they would write him a letter—like those the white soldiers in the war had received from their families—and would send it to him by a messenger. When the children came home, their father read their letters aloud to them. Ah-yoka had thought

119

of copying their letters. So, without looking at the signs from which Sequoyah was reading, they could read the same messages from their own pieces of bark and know that the words he repeated were those they had written down.

After the children went to bed, Sequoyah and Sally sat for a long time in the firelight, looking at each other, not speaking. Then Sally sighed a little.

"This is a very big thing," she said.

"It is too big for one man, or even for one family," Sequoyah agreed.

"Yes," Sally assented. "This must belong to all the people." She sat and thought for a moment. "How will you give it to them?" she asked him.

"I will have to show the Tribal Council and the chiefs," Sequoyah said.

"Then you will have to take it back to the Old Nation, in the east."

"Yes."

"How will you show it to them?"

"I can take the signs written on deer hide, as I brought them here."

Sally laughed. "Well, your load will be lighter going back. You brought a hundred signs west

120

with you, and you're taking only eighty-six of them east."

"Yes. Well, we all agreed I didn't need the other fourteen."

Sally was sober again. "But just showing the signs isn't enough. You will have to take somebody else who can read and write with you. Then you can send that person out of the room and play the same game that we do here at home with the children. Take one of them with you."

"Why don't we all go?"

"And let the farm go to pieces and miss a year's crops? We can't afford it, Sequoyah."

Sequoyah sat still in the firelight, considering. Once before he had gone away from home and left a wife in charge of a farm. When he came back, things had been bad, and it had seemed for a while as if his life must fall to pieces. But Sally and his first wife were different people— very different people. This time, he felt sure, he would not be making a mistake in leaving.

"All right," he said. "Which shall I take?"

"Take Ah-yoka," Sally said swiftly, as if she had made up her mind beforehand. "She's younger, and she's a girl. Surely people will believe, if they see that she has learned to read

121

The Cherokee capital was at New Echota,

and write. If a little girl can learn, anybody can. Besides, perhaps she will have a chance to see her mother and brothers while she's there. That would be a good thing. It isn't fair to let the child grow up without knowing anything about her own blood kin."

"Oh, that's silly. They don't care," Sequoyah retorted. Not for anything would he have admitted to Sally that sometimes he got homesick for Tessee and the other boys.

Going east was a longer, slower journey than going west, for this time they could travel down-

where a real town had grown up

stream by flatboat only to the mouth of the Arkansas, and that was the shortest stretch of the way. Beyond that point they had to walk most of the time. Once in a while they were lucky enough to hitch a ride for a short distance on a trader's or farmer's wagon.

The Cherokee capital was at New Echota, where a real town had grown up. There was a big, two-storied building where the National Council met; there was a gristmill and a trading post and the mission church and school which the Moravian Brethren from Pennsylvania had founded a few years before. And New Echota had

123

regular streets, with small one- and two-roomed cabins built along them. These were in use only a part of the year. The Council members and their families lived in these houses when the Council was in session, but closed them and returned to their farm homes at other times.

John Ross was chairman of the Tribal Council. He had a bigger place, with four rooms, and smaller cabins as quarters for his Negro slaves, inside a whitewashed snake-and-rider fence. There was a gallery—as the new word was—across the front of the house, and the center of the building was an open breezeway with two rooms on either side. Only John Ross didn't call it a breezeway. He used the elegant Virginian name, dog-trot, when he spoke of the open hall. Less well-educated whites, and many Cherokees, called the same passage a hog-trot.

Sequoyah went to see John Ross first of all, for a number of reasons. Ross was chairman of the Council and therefore the most important and influential man in the Cherokee Nation. Ross was more white than Indian by blood, and he had been well educated at Dartmouth College in the North. He read and wrote Latin and Greek, as well as English and French and Span-

124

ish, and naturally he spoke good Cherokee. He was the man, of all men, to know that it was possible to speak and write more than one language in more than one way. Besides all this, he was kindly and hospitable, and his house was always open to guests. Above everything else, he was Sequoyah's old and good and honored friend.

Ross heard Sequoyah out, when the tinker from the west told him why he had come east again. They sat together after supper, in the dog-trot, smoking their long-stemmed white clay pipes in friendly fashion.

"You really can read and write Cherokee?" the chief asked at last.

"I really can read and write it. So can my wife and children."

"So you can teach the skill to others?"

"I have taught it to my family."

"How long does it take you to teach it?"

"I don't know," Sequoyah said honestly. "I haven't tried to teach it to a stranger. The children have heard Sally and me talk about it for years—Ah-yoka heard me talk about nothing else long before that. I don't know whether it would take a stranger a day or a year or a week to learn it."

"It makes a difference," Ross said thoughtfully.

"I know it makes a difference," Sequoyah agreed. Again he thought about the matter. "How long does it take an Indian child to learn to read in the white man's school?" he asked.

"Three years," Ross told him, "but then, he has to learn the language, too."

"And that makes a difference, naturally."

"If anyone who wants to can learn it," remarked the chief, "and if he can learn it quickly, we can have our own schools—the schools of the Cherokee Nation. We won't need the missionaries to teach our children any longer, unless some parents want to send their children north to school."

"That will be good. When the missionaries teach the children to read, they also teach them a strange new religion."

Ross smiled. "It's a good religion, Sequoyah. I follow it myself, and so do all my family."

"Indians are Indians," Sequoyah insisted. "Indian religion is their religion." He shook his head. "Don't let's argue about that now," he said. "Let's stick to reading and writing."

126

"All right. How do you want to show your way to the Tribal Council?"

"I will go out of the room. Then you—or anyone else who wants to—can tell Ah-yoka what to write down. Then you can call me back, and I will read what she has written on the paper."

"Whatever we tell her to write?"

"Anything you tell her to write."

It was a big room, and it was packed with big men. Ross sat in a Windsor chair, at a walnut desk, facing the others. There was an open window behind him. A spray of wild rose had wandered across the sill and spilled its pink, flat-open blossoms down the wall, almost to the chief's shoulder. The big men were very quiet, staring at the little girl in the pink calico dress who stood before them, beside the chief. Quatie Ross, John's full-blood Cherokee wife, had given Ah-yoka the new dress, with white ruffles on its skirt and matching pantalets, that morning. It was Ah-yoka's first dress made of white man's cloth; always before she had worn homespun gray or brown linsey-woolsey. She looked very small and very pretty standing there, her straight black

127

*Ah-yoka and her father were going to show the Council
that they could read and write the Cherokee language*

plaits falling to her waist, her wide-open black eyes shining. She was as calm as the May morning outside the Council house, as unruffled as the spray of wild roses.

Sequoyah's own palms were wet, and the inside of his mouth and his lips were dry. He limped more than usual as he turned from the child's side and started toward the door at the back of the room. Just before he stepped outside, he paused and turned to look back. John Ross had handed Ah-yoka a real sheet of paper and a silver pencil tube holding a sliver of lead. She was examining them curiously, for she had never seen their likes before. Anger came up in Sequoyah's throat and closed his mouth in a hard line. What right had John and Quatie Ross to give the child new clothes—and paper and pencil to boot? She was strange to all those things! They would make her nervous—upset her—and she would forget how to read and write! All his work and all his life would be wasted.

He went far away from the Council house and stumped up and down in the dust of the open road, waiting, waiting, raging. He could hear nothing. There was no usual hum of voices from the men assembled inside the building; there

129

was no sound of a single voice raised in dictation. Even the mocking-birds and the bumblebees seemed to have fallen quiet, to be waiting with him to know whether Ah-yoka—and he—had succeeded or failed.

He reached the end of the town and swung on his heel before the last house, facing back toward the Council meeting. Someone was standing in the door of the Council house, beckoning, signaling to him with an upraised arm. Ah-yoka had done her part—or had failed to do it. Now it was up to him.

The outdoor stillness had crowded into the Council house. Not one man in the big room seemed to move, or even breathe, as Sequoyah made his way among them, back to the standing place beside John Ross. Ah-yoka turned her head and smiled up at him, holding out the piece of paper as she did so.

"Here is it, Father," she announced.

The neat characters darted about the paper like lizards, alive before Sequoyah's eyes. Ah-yoka had been very careful indeed, writing for the first time with paper and pencil. Then his hand steadied and he began to read, not trying

130

to understand the words, making himself pronounce only the sounds for the signs before him.

The stillness bound the room for a full moment after he had finished. Then the Council men were on their feet, pressing forward, trying to seize the hand John Ross had clutched and dropped. All the men were talking at once; some were cheering. Ross reached down and swung Ah-yoka, pink dress, white ruffles, dangling braids, and all, up on his desk and held her tight against his chest.

"Ah-yoka, gentlemen," he said when the first excitement had quieted. "Ah-yoka. She Brought It."

7
What It All Meant

This seems like a good place to stop the story of Sequoyah for a few minutes and take stock of his achievement. Was his work as important as he thought, as worthless as his first wife said, or somewhere in between?

Writing has been invented very few times in the history of the world. Our own alphabet has come down to us from the Phoenicians, by way of the Greeks, who gave it to the Romans, who taught it to the other peoples of Europe. Then it went west, and with each step of the journey to America the alphabet was slightly altered—new letters were added and old ones were discarded—until the dull old twenty-six characters that we know and take for granted jolted themselves down into a system for recording and transcribing the English language.

When our alphabet crossed the Atlantic with Columbus—who was, even for his day, a poor speller—there was no true system of writing anywhere in the New World. Remember the three great lacks of the Indians, which were mentioned in the introduction. They had no knowledge of the wheel. They had no knowledge of metal tools. They had no true alphabet.

It is true that the Maya developed, and later taught to the Aztecs, a system of recording that our scholars have not yet completely deciphered.

But the Maya system was what is called "rebus" writing. We see rebus writing in our newspaper advertising sometimes; it is usually made into a puzzle where a picture of an eye stands for the letter or the personal pronoun "I"; the letter U represents "you"; and a drawing of a winged insect is meant for the verb "to be." Rebus writing is a system using *pictures* for sounds, words, or ideas, and it is because the same picture can represent any one of the three that rebus writing is a puzzle to read. Because we lack the code key to the Maya drawings, we have not yet been able to figure out all their rebuses. Perhaps someday a scholar will know enough of the Maya language and the thought habits of the people who spoke it to understand what each Maya drawing stands for. Perhaps.

SOME OF THE CHARACTERS IN THE CHEROKEE SYLLABARY

Groups of letters they represent:

35. Queegh	40. Kaah	45. Taugh	50. Eeh
36. Quegh	41. Tsahn	46. Keh	51. Ooh
37. Sah	42. Sahn	47. Taah	52. Yeh
38. Quah	43. Neeh	48. Khan	53. Un
39. Gnaugh	44. Kah	49. Weeh	54. Tun

But Sequoyah, as we have seen, went a step beyond rebus drawing, to the development of a true writing system. What he invented was not an alphabet, actually, where each letter stands alone and can represent several sounds, depending on its association with other letters. His invention was what is called a syllabary. A syllabary presents more rigid meanings for its symbols than does an alphabet. That is, in Sequoyah's syllabary there is a single sign for "Sah," another for "Keh," another for "Un," another for "Yeh," and so on. Our alphabetic system uses *two* or *three* signs of each of these sounds. Sequoyah's system combined; the European alphabet separates.

So, if you want to speak correctly and accurately of Sequoyah's work, you will call his invention a "syllabary," and not an "alphabet," as many people who should know better still do.

Well, then. The thing is named. Was it important?

We have the word of all the Cherokees that it was. We have the word of all his people that Sequoyah was their greatest man. And we have the word of scientists and scholars that such a thing never happened again in human history. Never

135

before or after Sequoyah, anywhere in the world, did one man alone perfect a system for writing and reading *any* language.

Sequoyah had taught Sally and the children to read and write Cherokee, and to them it was a game. His next pupils were John Ross and the other members of the Cherokee National Council. They set aside all their official business, and with Sequoyah and Ah-yoka as their teachers, they went to work. Paper strewed the floor of the Council house; pencil points wore down and quill pens spluttered while the Council became literate in its own language. It took only three days for the slowest and most plodding Council member to learn to read and write Cherokee, and one of the first laws the Council enacted in Sequoyah's syllabary was that each Cherokee child should be taught the system.

Now it was as if a door were opened and light streamed into a darkened room. The members of the Council went out, and wherever they went, as they journeyed to their homes, they told the people they met of Sequoyah's invention. They showed everyone who listened to their words how to use the syllabary. Men left their plows, women their spinning wheels and looms, and

136

children their play, to learn to read and write. The first teachers scratched the characters of the syllabary in the dust of the roads, on the rails of fences, or, as Sequoyah himself had once done, on the leaves or bark of trees.

Sequoyah stayed in the East for a year, at the request of the Council. While he was there he trained teachers and he helped others put the syllabary to use. Later he watched while the eastern Cherokees became truly a people set free. And when he was ready to return to the West, he took with him a load of letters written by people in the Old Nation to their relatives and friends in the Nation West. As soon as the westerners learned to read, they would be able to reply.

He presented the system to the Council in 1821. Three years later, in 1824, Atsi, whom the missionaries had renamed John Arch, completed a translation of the Gospel According to St. John into Cherokee. In the following year, 1825, David Brown, a full-blood Cherokee, completed his translation of the rest of the New Testament.

Now an exciting thing happened. One of the great projects of the missionaries to the Cherokees had been to translate the Bible and other religious books, school books, and even some

137

stories into Cherokee. They wished to publish a newspaper and magazine that members of the tribe could read. They had originally planned to use an elaborate and rather clumsy method of phonetic transcription, using English characters, which had been perfected in Boston.

When Sequoyah's syllabary was adopted by the Cherokee Nation, one of the missionaries, Samuel Austin Worcester, who was in charge of the printing and making of books for the Nation, saw the new system and was greatly impressed by it. Worcester immediately decided that if books were to be printed in Cherokee they should be printed in the Cherokee system. English types had already been ordered for the Cherokee National Press, but at Worcester's insistence they were scrapped—melted down and recast—and Cherokee types were cast instead.

From its very beginning, then, the Cherokee system was both written and printed, and there was no difference between the forms of the letters used in writing and those used for printing. And from its very beginning the Cherokee National Press was the *Cherokee* Press, using Cherokee in the make-up of the first issue of the *Cherokee Phoenix,* which was published in 1828.

If you know any Greek mythology, you will remember that the Phoenix was a supernatural bird. When it grew old it burst into flames which completely consumed its aging body. Then from the ashes a young, powerful Phoenix arose, and soared to the skies again on strengthened wings.

So it was with the Cherokee Nation in the time of Sequoyah. In 1828 it had a national press, a national newspaper, and a national magazine. It had set up a system of national schools, with regular standards of teaching and learning. It was putting on paper plans for a national academy of higher learning and for a national museum.

All the achievements of the Cherokee Nation were as much Sequoyah's as any other one man's. And the Nation recognized the greatness of what he had done, and rewarded him with an income of $500 a year, derived from the working of a Nation-owned salt bed near Sallisaw. This was the first (and probably the only) purely literary pension ever awarded within the history and boundaries of the United States.

More important still, the Cherokee Nation recognized the fact that a man who was capable of such greatness in one part of his life was capable of greatness in other directions as well. Sequoyah was not a member of the National Council, but he was one of the Advisers of the Nation—what the Cherokees called one of the Old Beloved Men—and in that capacity Sequoyah made at least two trips to Washington. There he signed his name, in his own characters, to treaties setting the boundaries of the Chero-

Sequoyah made at least two trips to Washington

kee Nation. "George Gist," it is written in one place, and "George Guess" in another, as if the English-speaking secretary who made the transcription were uncertain as to the exact values of the Cherokee consonants.

"George Guest" he had been enrolled when he enlisted in the United States Army under General Jackson, and probably the English first name dated from that time. Sequoyah himself used it as little as possible. Whenever he wrote his own name he did so in the Cherokee characters that are best translated: The Lame One.

8
And West Again

The year Sequoyah and Ah-yoka spent in the Old Cherokee Nation was a busy one, full of strangers, full of adventures, full of honor and praise. But Sequoyah did not forget that one of his plans before he came East was to see his sons and to let Ah-yoka meet and speak to her brothers. As soon as the first hard work of teaching was over, the two of them set out from New

142

Echota for the Overhill country, riding on two neat-footed bay ponies the Councilmen had awarded Sequoyah.

The slopes of the hills were brown and dusty with midsummer as they traveled. Every fold of the earth, every rock that lay against the tall grasses, spoke to Sequoyah. This land was his; this earth was his home, in a way that the western country had never been and never could be. True, he had turned his back on the old Cherokee country deliberately. True, he had lived well and prospered moderately in Arkansas Territory. He had done the right thing in going there, he was sure. The Cherokees could not hold the Old Nation forever; they could not even hold it much longer. White men were pushing in against them constantly, and no laws of the Nation or treaties with the United States could hold the invaders back. It needed only for some one thing that the whites greatly wanted— gold, for instance—to be found on Cherokee soil. Then the dam would burst, and the white flood would pour across the land. . . .

They came to the stretch of country that lay between the Holston and the Tennessee rivers.

143

Here the curves of the earth were gentle and the light was softer still. Here the world was hushed and at peace in the afternoon light. A cabin stood in a clearing and the smoke from its chimney rose, curling ever so slightly, almost straight upward.

A young man near the cabin leaned his ax against a woodpile and came to meet the travelers. Ah-yoka sat on her pony, staring at him, but Sequoyah slipped to the ground from his saddle and limped forward, while the young man stared in his turn. The older was the first to speak.

"You are Tessee?"

"Yes."

"I am your father——"

He had never put in words, even in his most secret thoughts, what he expected his son to say. Whatever it was, it was not what Tessee did say. For the young man took the older man's hand and said in the old formal greeting, "Come in your house and be very welcome." He turned to his sister. "Get down, Ah-yoka. Come and meet my wife, and your new nephew. He was a week old yesterday."

144

Afterward they were all calmer than they had felt at first. They stopped all talking at once, and crying a little, and admiring the baby, although Sequoyah secretly thought that this first grandson of his deserved all the admiration anyone gave him. Ah-yoka, with her new sister-in-law directing her from her bed, found food and dishes and put a meal on the table. Then they all gathered around, and ate and talked and talked and ate. Afterward the sister-in-law had Ah-yoka bring the dishes and dishpan to the bedside, so she could help with the cleaning up. The two men went to sit on the woodpile just outside the door, where they talked some more.

"This is good country," Sequoyah said contentedly, looking around him.

Tessee nodded solemnly. "Good country indeed, Father. Too good to last."

"The whites?"

"The whites are coming in. They say that gold has been found in the Nation."

"Where?"

"At Dahlondega, in Georgia. It's a long way away from here, as the road winds."

"It's too close for comfort as the crow flies,

145

though," Sequoyah remarked. "Of all the whites, I think the Georgians have treated the Cherokees worst. If they want land and gold in the Nation, the Cherokees had better move. It's easier to give, than to give up."

"You're right, of course, Father. But where can we go?"

"You'll have to come out to the Nation West, and join those of us who have already settled there. The time will come—the time is coming—when you will all be forced to go. Better go willingly, boy."

"My wife is an orphan——"

"Do you want your son to be an orphan too?"

Tessee's eyes were fixed on the ground. "What can I do to earn a living in the West, Father?"

"How do you earn your living here?"

"I farm. I split rails for fences and shakes for roofs, and splints for baskets—I even mend pots and beat out knife blades or fix ax bits on handles once in a while——"

"Those are all things you can do in the Nation West just as well as you can do them here. You can earn just as good a living out there, doing the same kind of work."

"And have land enough to live on?"

The following spring they set out for the Nation West

"The Western Council will give you plenty of land to live on."

"We'll go back with you, Father."

So when they started west again the following spring, there were five of them. The other boys were all scattered and all married. Sequoyah and Ah-yoka had visited each of them, and invited them to make the trip to the West, but for their various reasons the boys refused.

But Tessee had traded work all winter with a wagon-wright, and so his wife and baby rode in a creaking oxcart. The cart was loaded with their household goods. This was not a covered wagon; covered wagons were still to be perfected in northern New York State. This was just an open, four-wheeled cart, with its load covered with a sheet of brown canvas which was spread neat and taut. But the wagon carried the table, the stools, the dishes, the pots and kettles, and the baby's cradle. There was even room enough, on a board laid as a seat across the front of the wagon box, for Tessee to rest when he grew tired of walking beside the oxen.

Sequoyah and Ah-yoka rode their ponies. Sometimes they went ahead of the slow creaking

148

of the wagon, and once, when they were out of sight of it, Ah-yoka spoke to her father.

"I'm sorry my mother is dead," she said. "I'm sorry she died before I could see her again."

"Try not to miss her, child," her father comforted her.

"That's what I'm sorriest about," said Ah-yoka. She reached forward and stroked the smooth skin on the pony's neck. "I don't miss her. It all happened too long ago. The first person I can remember—really remember—is you. And then, later on, Sally and Squirrel Boy. Sally is so good to me. No mother could treat me better. I never really knew my mother and I don't know how to miss her."

"Then try not to worry," Sequoyah advised. "Your mother loved you, and if, later on when you are more grown up, you decide that you have missed having a mother's love, blame me, not her. I took you away from her and kept you away from her. If you have ever lacked for anything, Daughter, it has been my fault."

But Ah-yoka shook her head without answering in words, and her father knew she meant that she had never knowingly lacked for anything.

149

9

The Last Journey

Life was very good to Sequoyah now. You remember that his pension was in the form of income from a salt bed. There he and his boys boiled down the water from a saline spring and made salt for sale to their neighbors and to travelers who came through the western Nation. They had enough work to keep them all busy and interested, but they could work freely, without pressure or tension, and so their work was a joy to them.

When he grew a little tired of the home place, Sequoyah always had a reason for a vacation. He could go through the Nation teaching or visiting the schools where he was always welcome to sit and listen to the children as they recited their lessons. He could go into the woods and watch leaves twist and turn on their stems or release their hold on the trees and drop, still twisting, to the ground. He had time to think about many things, and no one found it strange that he wanted to spend time thinking.

He was particularly thoughtful about the problem of applying his syllabary to other Indian languages. He talked to the Kickapoos and Shawnees; he talked to the Creeks, he talked to Choctaws and Chickasaws. Whenever he found a word in another language that was like a Cherokee word in sound or meaning, he made a special note of it.

In the back of his mind an idea moved slowly, dreamily. All the Indians he knew, all the Indians he had heard of from the earliest days, spoke and had spoken different languages. Yet as time went on Sequoyah became more and

151

more sure that somewhere, thousands and thousands of years before—before the beginnings of the long wanderings that sent them through the New World—all Indians everywhere must have spoken a single great language. And he hoped, he almost dared to believe, that his writing would be a way of discovering what that one language had been like.

He used every opportunity that came his way to try to discover the clues to the lost Indian tongue. His trips to Washington were made on tribal business, but when business was finished he found chances to talk through interpreters to the delegates of other tribes. Some of them were people who came from far and away to the west. In time he came to believe that those western Indians had not traveled as far over the face of the land as the Cherokees, for he could soon recognize words that many western tribesmen had in common. Perhaps their languages were purer, nearer to the ancient root language that he was convinced must once have existed. But not from the Osage or the Mandan, not from the Winnebago or the Hidatsa, did he discover the key, although he was sure that their tongues were related to one another and also to the language he had heard the southern Cheraw speak long ago. Indeed they were, for all these tribes belonged to the great Siouxan linguistic family.

No, Sequoyah decided at last, he would have to make a trip all by himself, or perhaps with Tessee and some other younger men. He would have to go west or south, to find more Indian tribes and listen to more languages, before he would have the knowledge he needed to identify the Great Indian Language. South—that was the way to go. South—into Mexico, the heart and center of Indian learning before the white men scattered the Indians and their languages over the face of the lands like blown leaves.

Coming back from a trip to Washington, he stopped to rest at John Ross's home near Park Hill in the Indian Territory, which is now a part of eastern Oklahoma. The whole Cherokee Nation had been moved west by the United States troops under General Winfield Scott in 1838 and 1839. Great had been the suffering of the people along the way. Quatie Ross had died on the Trail of Tears, one of nearly a third of the Cherokee Nation who had not lived to see the western country. John Ross had mourned her deeply and truly, but now he was married

153

again, this time to a white woman from New England.

Once, perhaps, Sequoyah would have said to the survivors of the terrible westward migration, "See. I told you so. It would have been better to leave your lands to the whites while you could, and to have come west of your own free will and in your own time, instead of being herded along the trails and rivers like cattle."

But Sequoyah was getting to be an old man now. He could not use the time remaining to him unkindly. When a man knew he had only a few years left to live, he knew also that he must spend them generously, in doing as much good— in being as good—as he could.

He sat on the gallery of the Ross home, looking out across the little gentle, rolling hills. The land here was shaped much as was that of the Old Nation, although it was smaller and softer. The Ozarks and the Cookson Hills were the Smokies reduced, hills small enough to hold in a man's hand as well as in his heart. He watched a dust cloud form itself down the road toward Tahlequah, the National capital. Out of the cloud a horse and buggy took shape. Presently

154

the carriage stopped before the gate in the picket fence John Ross had set around his dooryard.

A young white man jumped down from the buggy seat and opened the gate. He was half-way up the walk while his Cherokee driver was still tying the horse's reins to the hitching post. There was a step on the gallery behind Sequoyah. John Ross and his young second wife had come out, and were waiting to welcome the visitors.

There was much talk, chattering back and forth in English, with a sound like grackle clashing their beaks. Then Ross smiled and made an open gesture with his right hand toward the man beside him on the gallery.

"Sequoyah," he said, and went on jabbering away in English. The young white man's jaw dropped, and he stared. It must be a surprise, Sequoyah reflected, to be introduced to an elderly Cherokee who stood there with a clay pipe in his hand, with a flowered cotton shawl wound about his head like a turban, and wearing a long-tailed dark blue calico shirt made by the same pattern as an old-style buckskin hunting shirt. Just a plain, ordinary old Indian, in old-

155

fashioned Indian clothes. Still, the young white man leaped forward with his hand outstretched and seized Sequoyah's hand. Instead of laying palm against palm momentarily, as a Cherokee would have done, he clutched the hand greedily, as if he wanted to take it away from Sequoyah and make it his own.

"His name is John Howard Payne," John Ross said, and Sequoyah could hear the smile in his voice, a smile that did not show on Ross's face or in his eyes. "He comes from Philadelphia; he is writing articles for a newspaper there. He has heard of your work—naturally—and he wants to write an article about you."

"They all do," said Sequoyah. He was a little tired of talking; tired of telling the same story over and over. He looked at Payne, and the white man returned his gaze only a moment, then dropped his eyes politely, as if he were an Indian himself. "How long has he for listening?" Sequoyah asked, and Ross relayed the question.

"His time is his own," the chief said when Payne had answered. "He will listen to you when and where and as long as you like."

Sequoyah considered. This was a new experience. Usually white people wanted to stare at him, as if he were the eagle the soldiers kept caged in front of their barracks in Washington. They wanted to hear him say a few words or perhaps recite the Cherokee sounds in order, as the children learned them. Then the whites shook his hand—hard—and went away, and what they found to write about Sequoyah never knew. Perhaps they picked up gossip from the neighbors. But here was a man who said he had time and was willing to use it to learn things properly, from Sequoyah's own lips.

"Has he an interpreter?" Sequoyah asked John Ross, and again there was an exchange of English words.

"He says he has a linguister," Ross reported. Like Payne, the chief pronounced the word "linkster." "His driver can interpret for him."

Sequoyah turned to the young Indian, who stood at the edge of the gallery and who, so far, had not said a word. "What is your name, my son?" he asked.

"David Vann."

"Son of the David Vann who used to live at Spring Place, Georgia?"

"His grandson, Honored One."

"Time passes. Time passes, and when it leaves

157

it is gone! Who taught you to speak Cherokee, son? Your grandfather? No, he died on the trip westward, now I remember."

"My father and my mother. We were never allowed to speak English at home. I learned it from the soldiers and the settlers, along the Trail of Tears."

"You speak Cherokee well. Do you think you know enough English to translate my words?"

"I think I do."

"Good. Then tell Mr. Payne that we will talk tomorrow. I have nothing much to do all day."

David Vann translated Sequoyah's words, and Payne nodded his assent. The boy hesitated for a moment and then spoke again to Sequoyah. "Honored One, before we start the real work to-morrow, I would like a chance to listen to you. Will you talk to us for a little while this evening? It would give me a chance to get used to your voice, and to the words you use."

Sequoyah smiled slightly. "A good idea; the kind of idea your grandfather would have had. Yes, certainly. I think you should practice for an hour or so this evening, so that you grow accus-tomed to my way of speaking. We older people

158

know and use words that you youngsters are los-
ing, I'm afraid."

They sat on the gallery again after supper, and
in the warm dark, soft around them as a buckskin robe, Sequoyah began to speak. David Vann
listened to the old man's words, and Payne listened to the sound of his voice. John Ross and
his white wife, Mary, sat behind them and listened too. Mary was learning Cherokee from her
husband and she took every opportunity she had
to listen to other people speaking. Once in a
while there was a pause, when Sequoyah stopped
to think of the order in which things of his life
had happened; when he relighted his pipe;
when he stopped to rest in order to ease his voice.
Once, in such a lull, Payne asked a question, and
Vann answered it without turning his head.

"What do they say?" Sequoyah asked John
Ross.

"Payne wants David to interpret what you just
said, but the boy says he isn't ready. He just
wants to listen to you tonight."

The stars had moved a quarter-turn around
the sky before they all went into the house to
their beds. And morning came early, wakening

Sequoyah first. He had been to the pump and washed, rebound the turban about his head, and lighted the morning's pipe, before smoke rose from the kitchen chimney to show that the Negro cook was up and about and breakfast was on the way.

After the meal John Ross suggested, "There is an upstairs room, you know. Mary will be in the kitchen all morning, working. Why don't you take that room? Then if anyone comes to the house you will not be disturbed, and you can work right through the day if you want to."

"Good," said Sequoyah, and he waited while Ross repeated the words in English.

They went upstairs and settled themselves in the little room, whose window opened out across the river and the hills. Thoughts were moving in Sequoyah's mind, thoughts that followed on the words he had spoken the night before, like children following their parents. He had things to say, things that he wanted to say to young David Vann, who seemed to understand him and to think as he did. It would be good to say these things now. Perhaps, too, the white man, Payne, when he heard about the One Great Indian Language, might be able to help Sequoyah discover it. Payne was a man who traveled. . . .

"In order that you shall understand," Sequoyah began, "I shall have to go back to the beginning of things. I shall have to tell you a part of the history of the Cherokee people, of their long wanderings, and of the other tribes they met along their way, before I can tell you of my work, and of what it must lead to. . . ."

He spoke formally, as the older men always did in Council. This was not a small thing that he had to tell about. It was a great thing; a thing so great few people could understand it; a thing so great he had not even tried to explain it to most of his friends. Young Vann sat on a low stool, his legs crossed and his hands clasped around his upraised knee, listening and watching and waiting, gathering into his heart the thoughts Sequoyah offered him.

Sequoyah stopped to light his pipe, and Payne asked a question. Vann shook his head, and, as he had the night before, answered without turning.

"What does he say?" Sequoyah inquired.

"He wants me to interpret, but I have asked him to wait. Go on, Honored One. You spoke of

161

the time of great learning and power, when the Cherokees lived in Mexico. . . ."

All day Sequoyah spoke and all day Vann listened. The young man's face glowed, as if his mind were a lamp in which a clean flame had been lighted. Payne too listened; Payne smoked his own pipe and listened. Once Mary Ross came to the door of the room and lingered briefly. She went away, and when she returned she brought them bread and cold meat and buttermilk. Sequoyah spoke on, between bites, and Vann listened still, too entranced to be hungry, too enraptured to eat. Hour after hour, and the afternoon passed, and the sounds of evening rose through the house and reached them.

At last, in the gathering dusk, Sequoyah was silent. He had told the things that were of the greatest importance in his life; of the meetings and partings of tribes; of their friendships and their long enmities; of the need for all Indians to understand one another. He had spoken of the things the Indians shared, and had explained that there were many more facts and beliefs to unite them than to separate them. Above all, he had spoken of the need to find the Lost Indian Language, so that all Indians could communicate directly with one another. And Vann had listened and had understood.

Payne asked a question, and Vann, unthinking, answered him in Cherokee.

"I cannot tell you now. It is too great—too beautiful." And then, remembering, he spoke in English, "It is too beautiful—too beautiful." He led the way down the stairs and out into the warm twilight, still repeating, half under his breath, "Too beautiful—too beautiful."

When the visitors went away next morning, Payne's questions about interpretation were still unanswered, and David Vann still walked like a man in a dream.

Out of the words he had spoken that day, Sequoyah's plan took shape. It was the year 1844, and he was sixty-nine years old. He would not live forever, and he might not be able to travel far in a few years. He was an old man; he could not deny that fact, not even to himself on a warm day.

The children were grown. Ah-yoka was married; Tessee was managing the salt works, and he had trained Squirrel and the four sons of Sequoyah and Sally to help him. Sally herself was busy with the house and the grandchildren and the neighbors. They all had full and happy lives. They all loved Sequoyah, he was part of every life around him.

But he, like all men and even more than other men, had always had an inside life of his own. He, more than any other man, had to live that inner life through before his physical life ended. He had a dream, like the dreams of his boyhood, and now was the time, now when he was free of the needs of other lives, to follow it.

As soon as he told them his plan, Ah-yoka and Sally understood why he needed to go. He would be away from the Cherokee Nation for a while. He would go west, through the Cross Timbers that were the western boundary of the occupied Cherokee lands, and on through the Shawnee country to the plains where the Wichitas and Comanches lived. From there the land lay open and he could turn his trail south.

For Sequoyah was going to Mexico. There, he believed, he might find other Cherokees. Some of the Nation had hidden in the Smokies and remained behind in their old country when their kinfolk traveled the Trail of Tears. If Cherokees

164

had done it once, in his own lifetime, they might have done it long before. Perhaps, in some far, far-off day, Cherokees had lingered in Mexico, near the source of their knowledge. Sequoyah was going to look for them, to hear their language. And he would hear the speech of other tribes along the way.

Even more than he wanted to find those possible lost Cherokees, he wanted to search for the Mexican Indians who had taught the Cherokees the greatest things they knew—some of them things that the Cherokees still kept hidden from the white men. If he could find that tribe, whose modern name he did not know, he might find the Indian Language that was the root of all Indian languages. There, in Mexico, with all the other lost and forgotten parts of Indian greatness, he believed he could discover the end of his life's work.

Only Tessee protested against the plan when Sequoyah first spoke of it. Tessee could not let his father undertake the long journey alone.

"Come with me, then," Sequoyah told his son, and with three of Tessee's friends they prepared to set out.

165

"We'll be all right," Sequoyah told Sally when they said good-bye. "There are four of the youngsters, and Indians have always done everything by fours. We'll be safe."

"Come back safe," was all Sally said, laying her cheek against her husband's for a moment.

"We'll be safe," Sequoyah repeated. Tessee helped him to the saddle on the back of the white mule they had bought from a trader who came into the Nation from Missouri. "We'll be safe." But he did not say anything about coming back. That would have to be as the Powers willed.

The Worm, who went with his friend Tessee and Tessee's father and who knew English, told the story of their journey long afterward. He told how they made their way through the tangles of the Timbers That Crossed the Country. The Cross Timbers stretched from south to north and separated the Indians of the eastern woodlands from those of the western plains. The Timbers formed a wall of trees and brush that cut off travel from east to west, all the way from the Texas coast of the Gulf of Mexico to the rising land of the Ozarks in southern Missouri. Traveling through the Timbers, Sequoyah's party fol-

166

lowed the rivers when they could. They waded the streams when they must, and turned away from the rivers and hacked their way through vines and low-growing branches when the banks grew bluff.

They came out on the western edge of the Timbers at last, and camped for a night near the Council Springs that marked the future site of Oklahoma City. From there they turned south when they had rested the mule and the horses for four days. They went out across the great High Plains, following the bends and curves of the rivers, turning west and turning south again till low, barren mountains rose against the southwestern sky. There was a Wichita village on the north side of the range, and The Worm learned from a man who spoke English that those eroded hills were called the Wichita Mountains. The Wichitas were a village-living people. They welcomed the travelers into the cone-shaped shelters they made by tying bundles of thick prairie grass over willow frameworks. Again the Cherokees rested. They stayed with the Wichitas for several days, perhaps as long as a month. The Worm was an old man when he told the story of the journey,

167

and time and its days ran together in his mind.

But the Wichitas treated the strangers kindly and fed them well, with corn and beans and squash from their fields—not quite the same varieties as those the Cherokees knew at home, but like enough. The Wichitas gave them the meat of buffalo and prairie deer and antelope. The older men of the village sat with Sequoyah and said words over and over, so he could listen to them and write them down. Here in the Wichita village Sequoyah was very happy. He heard no words that could not be written in his Cherokee signs.

The Comanches helped them along the next stretch of their way. The Comanches were horse Indians, raiders and fighters who had no friends. The Wichitas were frankly terrified when a party of young Comanche men, coming in from a buffalo hunt, rode into the village. They fed them, even giving them the first watermelons from their fields, but not as gladly as they had fed the Cherokees.

But the Comanches were as curious as they were warlike. They became interested in the Cherokees and in their strange and different ways of dressing and speaking. The Comanches

168

were especially interested and amused by the Cherokees' clay pipes. They themselves smoked rolls of tobacco leaves stuffed into the hollow tubes of deer leg bones. They puffed the smoke straight upward, and Sequoyah laughed in his turn when he saw them. He called the Comanches and their pipes "Cloud Blowers." When one of the young men offered to trade, Sequoyah exchanged his clay pipe for a bone cigar-holder. The Comanche had not realized how delicate the clay pipe was, and they all had to laugh out loud at the look on his face when he struck the pipe bowl against the sole of his foot to get out the dottle, and the pipe stem snapped.

They were as curious as monkeys, and as chattering, those Comanches. They told how, ten years before, some of them had gone out with a party of Kiowas, south and south and south, through and beyond great snow-topped mountains, around cities and within sight of huge, high-towered churches that made clashing sounds sometimes. They had gone south and south and south, into a warm, moist world, where vines twined and clung and held them back as the vines did in the Cross Timbers.

But where the earth of the Timbers was red

The Comanches were as curious as they were warlike

and dry and crumbling, the earth of the jungle
was black and damp and sticky. The Comanches
were frightened and made the Kiowas turn back
after a night they spent in the jungle. Mysterious
people, who must have had great power, sat on
the branches over their heads, talking, talking all
night, and throwing sticks and leaves at the in-
truders. In the morning the Comanches watched

170

those people swing through the trees with their long, black arms and their longer, blacker tails, and disappear. So, they were frightened, and they made the Kiowas turn back.

Frightened or not—and, in a way, the Comanches boasted of their fright—they were the people Sequoyah was looking for. He made them tell again and again—with the young Wichita who spoke English interpreting to The Worm, who translated into Cherokee for Sequoyah—all the steps of the journey.

At last Sequoyah made up his mind. These half-wild Plains savages, men who ate meat raw in preference to having it properly cooked, men who went about naked except for a coat of paint and a buffalo hide, these Comanches who were so uncivilized they hardly seemed like Indians, had been to Mexico. He was on the right quest, for the Powers Above had sent him here to this village, where he could find the guides he needed to take him farther south.

They took him first around the eastern curve of the Wichita Mountains, to a camp of their own people. It seemed that even Comanches recognized some authority, for the young men

171

asked permission of their elders to make the journey south again. There was much talking and discussion about it; the women ran to and fro among the skin tepees of the camp, for the Comanche women seemed to have as much right to argue as their men. Then, at last, the matter seemed to be decided. The Comanche women began packing up bags of dried meat pounded with berries and sealed into cakes with melted fat. Some of the older women made moccasins for the travelers; not only a pair apiece to wear when they set out, but three more pairs for each young man to take with him. They made moccasins for their own young men and they also made them for the Cherokees.

Again they traveled to the south, and the exact route they followed was hard for The Worm to describe, when he told about it afterward. Those were the days of the Texas Republic, when its president, Mirabeau B. Lamar, was offering a bounty for every Indian scalp a white settler brought in to Austin. So the Comanches led Sequoyah and his party on a winding trail, away from towns and settlements and even farms, through the mesquite thickets that misted the surface of the Plains, along the beds of dry rivers, perhaps up the limestone escarpments of the Edwards Plateau and down again to the bed of the Rio Grande. Once they crossed the Great River of the North of the Arms of God, as the Mexicans called it, they would be safer, the Comanches explained, for they would again be in Indian country.

And so they went southward—with bends and curves to the east and to the west as the country demanded them—but always southward. After they crossed the Great River they turned eastward, to avoid both mountains and cities, into the Mexican state of Tamalipas. Here the Comanches left them and turned back toward the Plains.

Sequoyah was truly an old man now, and he knew it. He was tired. Travel was hard for him. He and his old white mule were both giving out, and a day came when supplies were running low. They were not far from a Mexican Indian settlement. He sent Tessee and the others into the little town of San Fernando—gone from the map now—to buy supplies, while he waited for their return in a cave overlooking a river.

173

Sequoyah had gone to sleep forever

He was tired, but he was excited, too. The young men had promised to persuade some of the Mexican Indians to come back with them. When they came, he would hear them talk. Would he understand what they said? Would he be able to write down their words? His hand was shaking so that he lay back on the earth floor of the cave.

And there, when Tessee and the others came back with the leading men of San Fernando, they found him. He sat facing the door, wrapped in his blanket, the eyes that could no longer see the river still fixed on its banks. He had gone to sleep forever, waiting to see his first Mexican Indians and to hear them talk. We know now, from what later scholars have learned, that he would not have found their language to be related to Cherokee.

In 1907, when the state of Oklahoma was admitted to the Union, the first statue that the new state erected in Statuary Hall in the United States Capitol in Washington, D.C., was that of Sequoyah, the Cherokee genius. Even before then, however, the greatest tree that grows in American soil, the *sequoia gigantea,* had been named for him. Some say that the tree is the greatest and

175

most appropriate memorial that could have been given to the "Lame Man of the Talking Leaves."

Index

Ah-yoka (She Brought It), 90, 93–98, 106–12, 114–15, 121, 136, 142, 148–49, 164
  and invention of Cherokee writing, 118–19, 127–31
  marriage of, 163
  reunion with Tessee, 144
Alphabet, 132–33
Arch, John, 137
Arkansas, 77, 113
  Sequoyah in, 116

Ball game, Cherokee, 45–50
Battle of Horseshoe Bend, 82
Beads, as trade items, 18–19
Bells, hawk, as trade items, 17
Bible, translated into Cherokee, 137
Blacksmithing, 54–56
Blowgun, 33–34
Bookkeeping, early, 24–25
Brown, David, 137

Carving, wood for, 29–30
Cherokee Nation West, 77, 113–14, 146, 150
Cherokee National Press, 138
Cherokee Phoenix, 138
Cherokees, ball game of, ceremonial, 45–50
  as craftsmen, 52
  vs. Creeks, 75–76, 82
  dreams important to, 38–39
  early, 4, 6–8, 11
    astronomical knowledge of, 7
    change in ways of living, 11
  crafts of, 8–9
  doctors of, 7–8
  farming by, 7
  food of, 11
  and Forerunners, 4
  mathematical knowledge of, 7
  Mayan influence upon, 6
  music of, 8
  priests of, 8
  wanderings of, 3–7
  and writing and reading, 8, 11
  encroachment by white men, 68, 76
  initiation ceremonies of, 39–40, 45–50
  language of, 111–13
  and missionaries, 67
  moved west by troops, 153
  as nation, achievements of, 139
  in Revolutionary War, 26, 66
  river ceremony of, 39–40
  syllabary of, 134, 136–37
  treaties with, 67–68, 78
  in War of 1812, 75–76, 82
  Western, 77, 113–14, 146, 150
  whiskey disapproved by, 16
  writing system learned by, 136–37
Chickasaws, 151
Choctaw language, 10, 58, 112
Choctaws, 151
Cloth, as trade item, 16
Comanches, 164, 168–72
Copper, 9, 53
  working with, 57, 59–60
Creek language, 112
Creeks, 75–76, 81, 151
Cross Timbers, 164, 166–67, 169

177

178

179